Atypical Plays for Atypical Actors

ATYPICAL PLAYS FOR ATYPICAL ACTORS

Selected Plays by Kaite O'Reilly

OBERON BOOKS
LONDON

WWW.OBERONBOOKS.COM

This collection first published in 2016 by Oberon Books Ltd
521 Caledonian Road, London N7 9RH
Tel: +44 (0) 20 7607 3637 / Fax: +44 (0) 20 7607 3629
e-mail: info@oberonbooks.com
www.oberonbooks.com

A catalogue record for this book is available from the British Library.

PB ISBN: 9781783193172
E ISBN: 9781783193189

Cover image from 'In Water I'm Weightless', National Theatre Wales 2012, photo: Farrows Creative.

For Phillip Zarrilli,
my greatest collaborator in theatre and in life.

Contents

Preface

Kaite O'Reilly is not a playwright. At least not in the way the role is commonly imagined in the UK. The playwright, we often assume, gives birth to a play in the confines of sparsely-furnished attic room, taking an idea, a character, a voice, on a journey in their mind, discovering a form to fit their theme, with careful reference to the canon of all that has gone before. And then, nervously, they hand their text over to directors, dramaturgs, producers and actors for testing, trying out, improving, and eventual staging. A playwright writes a play.

Kaite O'Reilly works in a very different way, with very different results. In the piece from this collection that she and I collaborated on, *In Water I'm Weightless*, the starting point was a vast collection of texts – *The 'd' Monologues* – from which we selected several to create the performance – with the ordering and editing decided in and around rehearsals. Crucially, this process of selection didn't grow from some ideal sense of what the piece should be, but was rather a response to the people in the room, the particular group of actors – Mandy Colleran, Mat Fraser, Karina Jones, Nick Phillips, Sophie Stone, David Toole – their skills, personalities and bodies. Some monologues were split between several performers, others repeated by different voices, meaning different things in the differing mouths and hands. There was no one right way to perform these words – there was, instead, a multiplicity of possibilities.

This embrace of multiplicity is central to Kaite O'Reilly's work. Just as there is not – except in our most limited imaginations – a 'typical' actor, so there is no 'right way to write a play'. The texts in this collection all share O'Reilly's rich, winding, melodious, Irish-inflected voice, but they couldn't be more different in shape, in tone, in theatrical behaviour. *Cosy* and *The Almond and the Seahorse*, seem, at first glance to be the most 'play-like', though each builds its structure partly from the world and bodies of its protagonists, *peeling* is a great triumph of intertextuality – a play built from commentary on a production we never see, while *the 9 Fridas* is an epic of experiment – weaving theatrical possibilities into every moment of the text – leaving the audience to make as many choices about what they have seen as the director and performers are given in interpreting the work. Not only is there no right way to stage this text, there is no right view of its central, multiply performed character, Frida Kahlo. We cannot know Frida, nor what O'Reilly thinks of her. We can only know how we respond.

There are few writers as articulate as Kaite when it comes to examining and explaining her choices. She is a proudly political person, whose own atypical body and mind have brought her to a deep understanding of the dangers of convention in any guise. These 'atypical plays' are a political project – a demonstration of what can be gained for theatre, and for understanding, when we throw away our assumptions about representation. The writer doesn't imagine something that the actor fulfils – the writer opens a world of possibilities that the actor enters with their own complex, resistant, bodies and selves. The triumph of the 'atypical actor' is not that they transform themselves into the character imagined by the writer, but rather that their ever-present individuality transforms the writing into something that was never imagined. As such, theatre dreams of a society where all members must constantly adapt to each others' difference. It's not an easy world, but it's endlessly creative.

And yet Kaite does not sit easily in the tradition of British political playwriting. Her themes are not a commentary on our society, in the tradition of a Hare or a Brenton, but rather a testing on stage of what a society, in all its pain, mess and beauty, can be. Her voice is never comfortable telling us how the world is, or how we might run it better. As poetic as she is political, her words slip quickly beyond any reference, towards the edges of our minds and sense, suggesting but never proposing. This is a politics not of programmes and proposals, but of lyrical possibilities.

Anyone looking in this collection for an answer to what an 'atypical play for atypical actors' should be like will end up only with questions. What if actors no longer 'play characters' but rather 'play with characters'? What if theatre language is not monologue or dialogue, but a shared, fractured endeavour? What if the writing of a play is just a first step towards making something extraordinary happen on the stage? The answers are not in these texts, instead these texts send us off on an exhilarating journey into the unknown. Kaite O'Reilly is not a playwright. She is an artist of possibilities. A great one.

John E McGrath
Artistic Director, Manchester International Festival

Introduction

In the 1980s, meetings and demos for the UK's Disability rights movement felt like an off-shoot of punk. It was creative, irreverent, defiant and visionary, with a ferocious energy I found intoxicating. Stirring speeches and passionate arguments challenged the second class status we disabled and Deaf people had been subject to. What had been labelled bad and wrong, damaged and to be pitied was transformed into the source of pride and power as we recognised a different kind of beauty. From these demos sprang protest songs and poetry – the roots of disability culture and cabaret.

Disability culture is subversive and innovative. It embraces all the possibilities of human variety, rejecting the narrow neuro-typical and corporeal notions of 'normalcy'. The work is often aesthetically and politically provocative. Being aware of the Social Model of Disability, which reveals disability as a social construct (rather as gender is), was liberating and empowering. These selected plays and performance texts, written from the start of the 21st century, 'answer back' to the moral and medical models of disability and attempt to subvert (often invisible) cultural norms and negative representations of disabled people.

PEELING

peeling was commissioned by Jenny Sealey for Graeae Theatre Company in 2000, as an experiment to discover what we might cook up together, Jen as director and designer, and me as playwright. It was different from our first collaboration, which was straight after college in 1986-88, when we acted opposite each other, playing lovers, in Tash Fairbanks's *A Private View*. In Graeae's Women's Company we toured across the UK, and internationally, even as far as Sarawak, bringing our sensory impaired Sign Supported English speaking lesbians to the towns of Borneo. At times my career as a disability artist has continued in the same surreal vein, crossing over my parallel career as a so-called 'mainstream' playwright.

Theatre is the study of what it is to be human, yet for so long the western theatrical tradition has illuminated only part of the stage, consigning many – like Alfa, Beaty, and Coral, my chorus characters in *peeling* – to the shadows. For millennia impairment has been used as a metaphor for the non-disabled to explore their fears of difference and the inescapable cycle of life. This might account for the ostracising of those whose neurological, cognitive, sensory and/or physical differences have been used as vehicles to scare, warn, define and explain the values and hierarchical structures of a particular society. Despite the western canon heaving with these symbolic representations, seldom have the writers been disabled or Deaf themselves, or written from those atypical embodied experiences. *peeling*'s metatheatrical performer-characters are well aware of this reality.

BEATY: *(Reading programme)* Apparently, according to the director's notes, we've all been deconstructed.

ALFA: I thought I was being a metaphor.

CORAL: For what?

ALFA: I don't know. I didn't think to ask what the motivation of my metaphor was.

peeling, written specifically for one Deaf and two disabled female actors ('Cripping up is the 21st century's answer to blacking up'), was originally produced by Graeae Theatre Company in 2002, 2003, and for BBC Radio 3. Its lively meta-theatrical form supports its central themes of war, eugenics, and a woman's control over her fertility, which are as relevant today as ever. It is one in a series of collaborations I have been fortunate to have with innovative Deaf women performers, directors, choreographers, and visual language specialists. I'm grateful to the generosity of Jenny Sealey, Jean St Clair, Denise Armstrong, and Sophie Stone, amongst others, whose influence has helped me as a hearing woman shape what I call 'Alternative Dramaturgies informed by a d/Deaf and disability Perspective.'[1]

1 Initiated when Arts and Humanities Research Council Creative Fellow at Exeter University (2003-06), further developed with the generous support of the International Research Centre 'Interweaving Performance Cultures', Freie Universitat, Berlin, where I was Fellow until 2016.

THE ALMOND AND THE SEAHORSE

The Almond and The Seahorse is a very different creature. Coined by 'Crip' poet Jim Ferris as 'O'Reilly's Trojan Horse', it is a 'mainstream' character-led realist drama about survivors of Traumatic Brain Injury, with subversive politics in its belly. A response to 'tragic but brave' depictions of those surviving head injury, and informed by personal experience, the play interrogates the reality of living with TBI, questioning who the 'victims' are.

IN WATER I'M WEIGHTLESS/THE 'd' MONOLOGUES

I first started exploring the form of the monologue with a Creative Wales Major Award from Arts Council Wales. This project became *The 'd' Monologues*, a series of solo pieces inspired by conversations I had with Deaf and disabled people across the UK in cafes, at their kitchen tables, on the phone, in hotel bars, in several parks, on skype, in railway station buffets and once on the bus. In these myriad locations I talked to strangers about their sex lives, their attitude to impairment, their dreams and ambitions, what angered and infuriated them about living in what was often described as a disabling world. Provoked by their anger and often wry amusement at the ignorant but well-meaning attitude of some non-disabled people, I started writing monologues, ensuring I never used anyone's story, as to do so would have felt like theft.

I wanted to recapture the spiked angry energy of the early disability rights movement as I watched from 2010 onwards David Cameron's Conservative government dismantle many of the equal rights and benefits we had won in campaigns over previous decades.

The 'd' Monologues ('d' for Deaf and disabled) created the basis of *In Water I'm Weightless,* a National Theatre Wales/Unlimited Commission, part of the Cultural Olympiad and official festival celebrating the 2012 London Olympics and Paralympics. Embedded in disability politics, aesthetics, and 'crip' humour, they are a montage of monologues that can be performed solo or as a chorus. For the production the director, my long-term collaborator John E McGrath, firmly put the selection of material into the actors' hands – a cast of six of the UK's leading Deaf and disabled performers. He encouraged them to choose monologues they connected with, but would never be considered for in a conventional audition. He cast across impairment, gender, age, and sexual orientation, often creating a choral sharing of what had been a solo, thereby working against the 'tragic but brave' isolated individual. Instead, the production presented multiple voices (visual and spoken), different perspectives, and a sense of community.

The text published here followed a very different process from my usual 'playwriting'. The words are mine, but the shape and form is a fusion, an equal co-creation between the playwright's dramaturgy, the director's dramaturgy, Nigel Charnock's choreography, and designer Paul Clay's soundscape and video design. It is a record of a score that came about in an explosion of generosity and collective innovation, and can be reinvented and restructured according to the design of any future maker or producer.

THE 9 FRIDAS

The performance text *the 9 Fridas* is a complex mosaic offering multiple representations of arguably the world's most famous female artist, Frida Kahlo, reclaiming her as a disability icon. Unperformed as yet in English, Phillip Zarrilli directed the Mandarin premiere for the closing production of the 2014 Taipei Art Festival, transferring to Hong Kong Repertory Theatre in October 2016.

COSY

The greatest of all my collaborators, Phillip Zarrilli, has worked as dramaturg or director on the majority of texts in this publication, including the most recent, a 2016 production supported by Unlimited. *Cosy* is a darkly comedic look at the joys and humiliations of getting older, and how we shuffle off this mortal coil. Eugenics and assisted suicide are the issues currently at the forefront of disability politics and societal debate. We all have to die, but what makes a good death? Three generations of a dysfunctional family explore their options in a world obsessed with eternal youth.

It seems clear that the complexities of our human condition will continue to provoke and claim my attention both as a woman and a playwright for many years to come. I look forward to the explorations.

Kaite O'Reilly, Llanarth, Wales, 24 January 2016.

peeling

'… *peeling* has all the deceptive simplicity and hopeful despair of a Samuel Beckett play. As in Beckett, the characters are tragic and comic, heartbreaking and ridiculous. As in Beckett the joke is ultimately on us… This is a major piece of theatre.'

★★★★ Lyn Gardner, *The Guardian*

'… a remarkably elaborate, imaginative and hard-hitting piece. O'Reilly's dialogue… has the punch and spareness of the late Sarah Kane's suicide-play, *4:48 Psychosis…*'

★★★★ Benedict Nightingale, *The Times*

'…a powerful and important piece of work… a minor feminist masterpiece … quietly ground-breaking …'

Joyce McMillan, *The Scotsman*

peeling was commissioned by Graeae Theatre Company. It premiered at Birmingham Repertory Theatre on 14 Feb 2002 prior to a national tour, with the following cast and company:

ALFA	Caroline Parker
BEATY	Lisa Hammond
CORAL	Sophie Partridge

Directed and Designed by	Jenny Sealey
Lighting by	Ian Scott
Dramaturg	Phillip Zarrilli

It was remounted by Graeae with a new cast and revised script, opening at the Assembly Rooms, Edinburgh on 18 September 2003, as part of the British Council showcase. It then made a second national tour, performing also in France and Republic of Ireland.

It was produced by David Hunter for BBC Radio 3 in 2003.

What follows is the updated script used for Forest Forge Theatre Company's national tour in 2011, directed by Kirstie Davies.

Notes

Three women emerging from outrageous, huge, gorgeous frocks. They are the chorus and part of the set design for a large production, which is going on unseen elsewhere on stage. The unseen parallel production is an epic visual piece about warfare through the ages: *'The Trojan Women – Then and Now'* – updated and with contemporary references. The three women have the occasional moment when they are 'on' in the parallel production, as tableaux-fodder and the chorus. Spotlight or floods signify these moments. The rest of the time they are 'unlit', able to relax and chat in the shadows, or comment on the scene before them. However, they are never completely 'off' and they use the devices of the theatre (narration, a form of audio-description, choral speaking, sign interpretation) even when there is no apparent audience. They bicker, play, interrupt – and share the above devices – when one stops, another takes up that role/device. They are constantly shifting and changing, sending each other up, 'ruining' each other's 'moment', taking the piss, passing easily between the formal 'roles' they play i.e., 'acting' (telling stories, being a narrator/audio– describer) and 'being themselves' (the chat and heckling). They obviously lie at times (for example in Scene 1, when Beaty & Coral pretend not to understand what sign language is, they are using SSE). As the play goes on, they change costume, simplifying, stripping down as the parallel unseen production becomes more modern and their stories become more personal and painful. By the end, they are peeled right down to simple underclothes: vests and pants.

A.D: Audio Description
SSE: Sign Supported English
BSL: British Sign Language

Where specified as being audio description (A.D), the speaker clicks into a different style of presentation – slightly more formal perhaps. It should fit comfortably and seamlessly into the dynamic of the dialogue/ scene, but be done with attention to the audience. Later, when used ironically by the women to comment rather than just describe, it should be layered with meaning accordingly and have a less neutral tone.

Characters

One Deaf and two disabled female members of the chorus of *The Trojan Women: Then and Now*

ALFA
calls herself an actress. She is fiercely independent, eccentric and slightly puritanical. She is Deaf and uses sign language (both BSL and SSE).

BEATY
calls herself an actor. She is feisty, a real beauty, and often in great pain.

CORAL
calls herself a performer. She is small and looks very fragile, but has a ferocious, inquiring mind. She uses a powered wheelchair.

One

Darkness.

The stage is suddenly filled with floodlight. Three large mounds are visible – huge dresses, with women sticking out of the top. Two, CORAL *and* BEATY*, are in performance mode – poised, highly theatrical – the third dress is empty. As the two women realise there is a vacancy and begin to lose their focus, sudden blackout.*

Five seconds pass.

The stage is suddenly filled with floodlight. Three large mounds are visible – all three dresses are inhabited. ALFA*, the latecomer, is slightly flustered. The women are static, artificial, poised in a series of tableaux.*

As Chorus in a strong post-modern production of 'The Trojan Women– Then and Now', they speak/sign to the unseen principles on stage (Hecuba and Andromache), as well as to the audience.

Chorus

ALFA: Raise your head from the dust.

BEATY: Lift up the throat.

ALFA: Sing.

CORAL: Hecuba: This is Troy, but Troy and we are perished.

BEATY: Woman: This is the world, for the verse of destruction you sing is known in other lands.

ALFA: Are we not hurled down the whole length of disaster?

CORAL: Throughout history, no change.

BEATY: Troy will be given to the flame to eat

CORAL: Sad birds will sing for our lost young

BEATY: The city will fall

ALFA: A horse with its lurking death will come amongst us

CORAL: Children will reach shivering hands to clutch at their mother's dresses

BEATY: War will stalk from his hiding place

CORAL: We will be enslaved

ALFA: We will die in our blood

BEATY: The same, the same, through the long corridor of time.

(Beat.)

CORAL: Gone will be the shining pools where we bathed

BEATY: Our children will stand, clinging to the gates, crying through their tears

ALFA: Know nothing. Look for disaster.
Lighten your heart.
Go stunned with terror.

(Beat.)

CORAL: I lived, never thinking the baby in my womb was born for butchery…

(Long pause.)

A shift in style. The intensity of lights dip, indicating the women are 'off' and therefore 'themselves' – professional actors who have been performing the chorus characters.

BEATY: *(To ALFA.)* So where were you? I turn round in the tableaux and there's an empty bloody dress beside me..!

ALFA: I got stuck, having a fag in the loo. You know how far backstage it is.

CORAL: No, I don't, actually. Thanks to the architect's love of stairs I've never managed to make it back bloody stage. I have to cross my legs and hope for the best. Through the whole epic. All four hours of it.

BEATY: You must have very developed pelvic floor muscles, then.

ALFA: What?

CORAL: You gave me a right turn, the lights going up and you not there.

ALFA: How d'you think I felt? First time in my life I've missed a cue. I'm a professional. Things like that don't happen to me.

CORAL: They did this time.

ALFA: First and only.

BEATY: They'll dock your wages.

ALFA: So I'll speak to the Equity dep'.

BEATY: Director won't like it.

ALFA: It won't happen again.
I'm sorry, all right? Beaty? Coral?
(BSL only.) Sorry.

CORAL: *(A.D.)* Alfa signs 'sorry' – her right hand drawing concentric circles over her left breast.

ALFA: I promise you, it'll never happen again.

BEATY: Yes, because you'll never work again.

(Beat.)

Every night this play.
Every bloody night this play.
Every night this bloody play. It gives me a headache.

The performers relax slightly, stretch in their cumbersome dresses. CORAL takes out a Tupperware box.

CORAL: Biscuit, anyone?

BEATY: *(A.D.)* Coral offers Hobnobs from her Tupperware box. *(As self.)* No thanks.

ALFA: The wardrobe mistress'll kill you if she catches you eating in costume. These frocks cost a fortune.

CORAL: Though quite what significance they have to wars ancient and modern is beyond me.

BEATY: Oh, I dunno… Every day's a little battle…it helps if you face it correctly attired.

ALFA: And a bit of luxury can't do any harm. Life's hard enough as it is. I quite like a touch of sumptuous padding.

CORAL: I feel more like a clotheshorse than a commentator on war.

BEATY: It's probably meant to be ironic.

(She takes out a programme and studies it.)

That's what they usually say when they bung together classic texts with contemporary stuff. Post-modern and ironic.

ALFA: *(A.D.)* Beaty refers to a theatre programme for *'The Trojan Women – Then and Now'* which she handily has under her skirts.

BEATY: *(Reading.)* Apparently, according to the director's notes, we've all been deconstructed.

ALFA: I thought I was being a metaphor.

CORAL: For what?

ALFA: I don't know. I didn't think to ask what the motivation of my metaphor was.

They look at ALFA, then the stage before them. Pause.

ALFA: Oh, here we go…

CORAL: *(A.D.)* The extras and unseen chorus…

ALFA: *(Interjecting, sign only.)* That is, us…

CORAL: *(A.D.)* … stare at the stage and the performance going on before them.

Several beats as they 'watch' the action of the play happening before them

BEATY: I hate this bit.

CORAL: Uummmmm.

BEATY: Pretty slow moving.

CORAL: Uuummmm.

ALFA: 'Interesting' interpretation of Hecuba…

CORAL: Uuummmm.

Several beats.

BEATY: Though she is very good.

ALFA: Yes, she is, she's very good.

BEATY: Marvellous.

ALFA: Really

CORAL: Uummm.

(Beat.)

BEATY: Though I could do better

ALFA: Given the chance

CORAL: Given the chance

BEATY: Given the chance I could definitely do better…

They sigh, attention begins to wane. CORAL puts away her biscuits safely under her skirts

CORAL: They sit.

BEATY: They sit.

(Beat.)

ALFA: We're like sitting ducks, stuck here in these crinolines. Or three lonely nuts on a coconut shy, waiting for the missiles to knock us from our plinths.

BEATY: *(To CORAL.)* I find it best to ignore her.

(Beat.)

ALFA: My mother'd say this was money for old rope. Us sitting here. Though she doesn't quite understand how demanding it is.

(Beat.)

CORAL: It can be taxing.

ALFA: To stay in the moment. Focused. Ready for the cue.

BEATY: *(A.D.)* We look at her accusingly. Alfa flushes, recovers, continues.

ALFA: The chorus to *The Trojan Women* is central.

BEATY: Which is why they've left us, shoved at the back, unlit, onstage.

(Beat.)

ALFA: It's a noble profession.

BEATY: I always wanted to go on the stage.

CORAL: And if we're going to be looked at, anyway, we might as well get paid for it.

BEATY: Did your mother tell you that?

CORAL: No. Did yours?

(Beat.)

ALFA: *(As storyteller.)* Once, once… Once there was an ancient city…

BEATY: She's off.

ALFA: Excuse me…? I'm rehearsing.

(As storyteller.) An ancient city set high, high among…

ALFA speaks quietly, then continues signing the story, not using voice.

BEATY: She does this every night… Every bloody night, as if she doesn't know it by heart already…

CORAL: Ooh, look! She's doing that lovely stuff with her hands!

BEATY: The Director will kill you if he sees you doing that.

ALFA: He wouldn't understand anyway. This is how it should be done.

BEATY/CORAL: Oooooooh.

ALFA: And whilst the principles are warbling on about their fate and the pity of war, I'm going to keep my mind fresh and creative and on what I'm supposed to be doing here, thank you very much.

CORAL: *(A.D.)* Beaty's eyes roll to the heavens.

BEATY: *(Mimicking ALFA.)* 'I'm a professional, how d'you do? Have a good look, I don't think you've met my kind before.'

CORAL: *(A.D.)* A cool, cruel glance passes between them. Alfa raises a finger.

ALFA: Up yours, lady.

BEATY: Will that be in the Sign Language dictionary?

ALFA: Once, once there was an ancient city, high, set high among the olive grove and almond orchards…

CORAL: And anyway it's terraces.

ALFA: What?

CORAL: Olive terraces. Set high, high among the olive terraces.

ALFA: That's my line.

CORAL: Well they'll take it away from you unless you say it right.

ALFA: Are you after my lines?

CORAL: No. I've got my own. But if you can't remember them or get them right…

ALFA: How do you know my part, anyway?

BEATY: *(A.D.)* A glint of suspicion enters her eye.

CORAL: I've heard it a hundred times!

ALFA: No you haven't!

CORAL: Have!

ALFA: Why are you learning my lines?

CORAL: I'm not!

ALFA: You're after my part! You're after…

BEATY: *(A.D.)* A poison dart of a look whizzes across the stage – an arrow wwhhhissshhhh – embedding itself firmly into the forehead of Coral, the possible role stealer…
The result? …sudden silence.

ALFA: Thank you.

Once, once there was an ancient city, high, high among the olive *terraces* and the almond orchards – an ancient city of women and children

BEATY: *(Overlapping.)* It'll have a bad end, wait and see. The ones with women and children always do.

ALFA: Ssh! An ancient city of women and children – fatherless families wandering –

CORAL: – Anyone seen *EastEnders* recently?

ALFA: …fatherless families wandering the maze of narrow cobbled streets…

CORAL: Boorrrriinnnggggg…..

ALFA: *(To CORAL.)* WILL YOU STOP IT!!!!????

BEATY: *(A.D.)* Flames blaze in angry eyes – Alfa's mouth scowls, the lips pucker... *(As self.)* really quite ugly, actually.

ALFA: AND YOU BEATY!

BEATY: Sorry.

ALFA: Christ!

BEATY: I was just trying to…

CORAL: *(A.D.)* Her gaze drops, cheeks slightly aflame.

ALFA: Yes?

BEATY: I was trying to…

CORAL: *(A.D.)* Beaty's teeth nip on her lower lip, pinching, bloodless…

ALFA: What?

BEATY: Audio-describe it.

CORAL: *(A.D.)* She tosses her head, looking defiant.

ALFA: Audio – ?

CORAL: DESCRIBE IT, idiot!
(Aside, to BEATY.) Bloody hell! She's away with the fairies, you know. Can't keep up. No brain – just mammaries on legs.
(To ALFA, as though no interruption.) Audio describe it.

ALFA: And why would you do that?

BEATY: Makes it more interesting.

ALFA: Only if you can hear.

BEATY and CORAL continue, oblivious to ALFA.

CORAL: I feel quite creative, actually.

BEATY: Yeah – I know what you mean.

CORAL: It's describing, innit?

BEATY: Yeah.

CORAL: Like – like painting the scene in visual images that the listener can absorb and internalise and – from spoken words – build that special visual world right inside their own head – in the heart of their imagination…

ALFA: Bollix to it, then. It's no bloody good to me.

BEATY: Yeah, but then you do all that lovely stuff…

ALFA: What?

BEATY: Y'know – all that lovely expressive stuff – with your hands…

ALFA: Sorry?

CORAL: Oh yeah – I know what you mean – that lovely sign-y thing…it's lovely.

BEATY: Really…

CORAL: …Yeah…

BEATY/CORAL: …Lovely!

CORAL: Lovely stuff when you wave them around – your hands – in the air – like…like…

BEATY: …like disco dancing

CORAL: Yeah…

BEATY: *(Starts singing and 1970s disco-dancing.)* D.I.S.C.O

CORAL: D.I.S.C.....

ALFA: *(BSL only.)* Fuck off! Yes….true…Fuck off!

CORAL: *(A.D, simultaneous with the above signing.)* Alfa signs ferociously –

BEATY: *(As self, interrupting.)* Viciously –

CORAL: *(A.D.)* – Beaty and Coral try to translate.

ALFA's following speech is presented in BSL/visual language only, with no voice. Simultaneously, CORAL and BEATY try to translate what ALFA is signing.

ALFA: Fuck off. Fuck right off the pair of you. Cows. Moo. Go away and milk yourselves. Squeeze yourself dry of that cynicism and ignorance. Prats. Christ knows how I manage, stuck here with you two. I won't do it again.

CORAL: *('Translating' simultaneously.)* Slap hands…slap hands together

BEATY: *(Simultaneously.)* Fuck…fuck-fucking

CORAL: Cow…noise they make…

BEATY/CORAL: Moo…moo…

CORAL: Touch breast…

BEATY: Tit! Milk cow…

CORAL: Milk ourselves?

BEATY: Milk tit fucking cow!

CORAL: Stupid!

BEATY: Milk tit fucking stupid cow!

CORAL: Fish!.. Shape hands make when…

BEATY: No..no no never…

CORAL: …Not?

ALFA has finished her signing.

ALFA: Amateurs. Bloody amateurs.

BEATY: Did you know an avocado stone crushed and combined with yoghurt, makes an invigorating and exfoliating shower gel?

CORAL: Did you know chocolate is a gift from the gods?

ALFA: Did you know we just had our lighting cue?

Theatrical lighting/floods on. The women pose, high theatricality, then go into chorus performing mode.

Chorus

CORAL: Women of Troy, this is not just your story.

BEATY: Hecuba and Andromache, this infamy has been well read.

ALFA: It has been told and re-enacted, made flesh as the sword marries the bone

CORAL: in that city

BEATY: in that village

ALFA: in that settlement, high, up in the hills

CORAL: low in the valley

BEATY: out in the bush

ALFA: deep in the city

BEATY: women and children

CORAL: waiting… for that feared-for smoke on the horizon. A smudge at the point where earth meets sky.

BEATY: Like a swarm of locusts

ALFA: choking the air

BEATY: beating down between heaven and earth.

ALFA: Fire

BEATY: Smoke

CORAL: Pestilence

ALL: Men

ALFA: marching forward with their uniforms

BEATY: and their machetes

CORAL: and their orders

ALFA: to rape

BEATY: to pillage

CORAL: to conquer

ALL: destroy

BEATY: slash and burn as they advance, burning the crops, killing the children

ALFA: dismembering limbs

BEATY: detaching achilles heels so the survivors can't run away, and so enabling the slaughter to continue, tomorrow.

CORAL: Taking the women for

ALFA: entertainment and pleasure

BEATY: and preferably impregnate them and kill off the line.

ALFA: Woman's body as battlefield

(Beat.)

BEATY: Rape as a war tactic

(Beat.)

ALFA: Mutilation as a reminder

(Beat.)

CORAL: Thank god that doesn't happen now.

A brief silence.

CORAL: In certain towns they chose to leave the dead where they fell and kept them so as remembrance – a memorial of scattered bodies – family members…neighbours…the school master… midwife…

BEATY: I had gone away that day, walking through the bush to the medical centre. I went alone. My little brother cried to join me, but I was a grown girl, on serious business. What use would he be to me? I made him stay home. When I returned, our soldiers stopped me from going to my village. They said there had been a massacre. A rival tribe. There was one survivor. People were hanging from the trees. Others lay in a pile of bodies in the schoolhouse, where they had been taken to be slaughtered.
My brother was in the schoolhouse.
He was curled, on his knees, covered by the body of my Mother who had tried to save him.
They had been butchered.

The survivor was me.

ALFA: *(A.D.)* The lights change. Ladies and gentlemen: a brief interlude.

Pause. The lights change. The women are 'off', now 'themselves'.

CORAL: I don't think I like this play very much.

BEATY: *(A.D.)* She shivers. Somewhere, big boots are walking over her grave.

CORAL: Don't.

ALFA: *(A.D.)* Alfa disappears from out of her dress

ALFA unstraps herself and disappears inside her huge tent-like dress.

BEATY: What's made you squeamish all of a sudden?

CORAL: Nothing, nothing, I, what!? Do you think something's different?

BEATY: No.

CORAL: Good, because there isn't.

BEATY: *(A.D.)* Beaty climbs out of her dress, taking her sewing kit with her.

CORAL: You know how sometimes when a show opens and it's been running a while and you get used to it and you go onto auto-pilot a bit…?

(A pronounced pause.)

(A.D.) Beaty avoids my eye, threading her needle, reluctant to admit she knows what I'm talking about.

BEATY: …Maybe…

CORAL: I know you're not supposed to go on autopilot, but…. I've just crash-landed…

BEATY: *(A.D.)* Coral struggles, pulls a face.

CORAL: …I…

BEATY: *(A.D.)* Her eyes hook into mine, urgent with meaning, but unfortunately I haven't got a bloody clue what she's talking about.

(As self.) What?

CORAL: I'm feeling it more. I've done it a hundred times, the mouth moving, words coming out, but I…I'm feeling it more…and… I don't like it.

BEATY: Just don't let it get to you.

CORAL: But some of the stories, the modern ones, they're…

BEATY: You think too much. Feel everything too much. Travel light. Go naked. Chill.

CORAL: Doesn't it get to you?

BEATY: No. 'Cause as an actress, I'm a carnivore – I like strong meat.

So the stories are full-on…Would you rather be in musical theatre?

CORAL: No!

BEATY: Well then…

CORAL: …but…

BEATY: What!?

CORAL: Well, I don't know…just sometimes… I'd like to do something…upbeat –

BEATY: Fantasy?

CORAL: No – positive. Uplifting. With a happy ending.

BEATY: Yeah. Fantasy.

ALFA throws open the 'doors' to the front of her skirt.

ALFA: Who'd like some soup? Some lovely cold Gazpacho?

BEATY: *(A.D.)* Alfa appears from inside her dress, with some vegetables, a bowl, and her blender.

ALFA: I never go anywhere without my blender.

She revs up her blender.

Hand-held, runs on batteries, hugely versatile…a lifesaver.

BEATY: *(A.D.)* She begins making Gazpacho.

ALFA starts chopping/grating vegetables from her mini kitchen inside her costume.

ALFA: Well, while there's a lull in the action, we might as well make the most of it. And that useless stage manager isn't going to bring us any refreshments. He's terrified of me. I'm sure he thinks 'Deafness' is catching.

BEATY: It is, if you're close to his ear and you shout loud enough.

CORAL: Beaty, would you mind sorting out my special cushion? It's hidden under my skirts.

BEATY: All right. *(She gets out a child's rubber ring.)* And I suppose you want me to blow it up?

CORAL: If it wouldn't be too much bother…..

BEATY: *(Between puffs of breath.)* You can get proper inflated cushions, you know. You don't have to use a kiddie's swimming ring.

CORAL: But I like the duck's head.

BEATY: It's probably a fetish – into rubber…

CORAL: You can talk! Sitting there in the intervals with your needle and thread.

BEATY: But that has class. Dame Judi Dench does embroidery when she's waiting between scenes.

CORAL: But I don't think she's customising her knickers.

ALFA: *(A.D.)* Alfa busies herself with chopping vegetables.

CORAL: *(A.D.)* Beaty shoves the rubber ring under Coral.

(As self.) Watch it!

BEATY: *(A.D.)* Beaty takes out some sequins and risqué lingerie. Coral notices Beaty's G-string–

CORAL: *(A.D.)* Largely because she's waving it around – some would say showing it off – generously displaying its crotchless nature…

BEATY: What can I say? Life's short: enjoy…

CORAL: Moonlighting, are we? I've heard you can earn, oooh, ten quid an hour in some of the booths in Soho, if you're lucky.

BEATY: Piss off, you're only jealous.

(A.D.) Smiling with anticipation, Beaty busies herself with choosing and sewing a sequin onto her evening attire.

CORAL: What's the occasion?

BEATY: I've a new boyfriend.

CORAL: Is he lush?

BEATY: Gorg'. You can see him yourself. He's picking me up at the end of the show and I do so like customising what I wear to bed.

CORAL: *(A.D.)* She continues with her adult-rated needlework. Coral squirms on her rubber ring. She wriggles, sighs with contentment. *(As self.)* I'm a martyr to haemorrhoids.

(A.D.) She sits with great contentment, looking about her, watching her industrious colleagues

(As self.) Make do and mend.

Preferably with cat gut.

My body is criss-crossed with scars like a railway track. Like Crewe station, seen from the air: Single tracks, with no apparent destination; major interlocking junctions, where intercity, sleepers and local lines all connect. Puckering scar tissue, hand-sewn with careless, clumsy stitches. I like to finger it, trace the journeys. That unborn skin: smooth, intimate – the coral-pink colour of mice feet.
It's beautiful.
I love it.
Given the choice, I'd never have it any other way, now.

(Pause.)

Are you listening, Mother?

(Pause.)

Do you hear me, Mother?

Several beats. ALFA, still preparing her soup, uses her blender as punctuation during the following:

ALFA: Mine used to warn me about men.

(As her mother.) 'You keep your hand on your ha'penny. You'll have to, if you want any kind of chance with a man. It's bad enough you being damaged goods. He'll not want you if you're second-hand, thumbed through and used already.'

CORAL: Ouch!

ALFA: I didn't pay any attention, though. You wouldn't, either, if you saw the cardigans she wore… But bless… I love my Mum…

CORAL: *(A.D.)* Beaty and Coral exchange a look of…

BEATY/CORAL: *(A.D.)* Envy.

BEATY: *(As her mother.)* 'You have to entice; you have to beguile. Put it all in the shop window Beatrice, though god knows you have little enough. Put yourself on special offer, dear.'

CORAL: Mothers…who'd be one, eh?

BEATY: They love to maim.

ALFA: But they think it's for our own good. Tough love. They're trying to help.

BEATY: Absolutely. Because we don't want to get too big for our boots, do we?

CORAL: And we mustn't aspire for other things… We have to be kept in our places.

BEATY: *(As her mother.)* 'Keep your aim low and you'll never be disappointed…You have a short shelf life, Beatrice, though you'd never know by looking at you. So keep smiling dear, and remember, it's quality of life, not quantity.'

CORAL: She's got a way with words, your mother.

BEATY: When they buried her, I had the greatest temptation to laugh down into that hole they were putting her in: 'So who was it survived the longest, then?' She was convinced she'd see me out.

CORAL: Was it sudden, then?

BEATY: For her, yes. Had no idea she was going. But I knew. To the tick. It's a talent I have – I've been thoroughly trained in it – to sense time passing and my old mate, the grim reaper, stalking close behind. All my life, thanks to my mum, I've felt the tip of his scythe touching the nape of my neck. My mother was so focused on that, waiting for me to croak, she didn't notice the big fingers come to snuff her out. So I buried her. There's not many with 'reduced life expectancy' can say that. It's an achievement. There's not many like me can press the earth down on their mother's face. Stamp on the grave. Put a layer of concrete over so she can't rise again.

I joke of course.

CORAL: Of course.

BEATY: Though she was the joker in our family. She'd call me into the bathroom and make me stare at her face. She was getting deep crow's feet around her eyes – she hated it – and the skin around her jaw line was beginning to soften – sag a bit – her face covered in fine hairs, like the fur of a peach. And she'd cradle her face in her hands and stretch back the skin so the wrinkles would disappear and she'd say: 'That's what I looked like when I was 16. You're lucky, Beatrice. Just think, you'll never have lines on your face like me – you'll never see your features blurring, you'll never suffer from the ravages of age. You're so lucky, Beatrice. You're so lucky you'll die when you're young. You're so lucky you'll never live to be old.'

(Several beats.)

Has anyone got any neurofen?

CORAL: Are you starting?

BEATY: I'm in the most terrible pain.

ALFA: You look pretty crap.

BEATY: That's the pain.

CORAL: You want to eat bananas when you're on your period.

ALFA: You do look crap.

BEATY: I can't help it.

ALFA: Ever heard of make-up?

CORAL: They're rich in potassium, which is exactly what you need

BEATY: I look crap even when I wear make-up.

CORAL: Or Evening Primrose oil, that's good.

ALFA: You look crap.

BEATY: I look so crap because I'm in such pain.

CORAL: And star fruit. That's the new one.

ALFA: I have to have an operation.

CORAL: Yeah, well I'm on my period.

ALFA: And the pills I have to take…

BEATY: I shit pills. They shoot out like coins from a slot machine in Vegas, just chug chug chug, all nudges and triples. It's the amount of tablets I have to take. For my pain. When I walk down the road I rattle.

ALFA: You rattle? I'm like a broken washing machine. On spin.

CORAL: Yeah, but at least you don't have your period.

ALFA: I am a wreck. In emotional and physical pain.
I am embodied pain.
I am the physical embodiment of emotional and physical pain.

CORAL: I get body cramps. Even my hair hurts when I'm having my period.

BEATY: I lose my vision.

ALFA: I lose my hearing and I'm Deaf.

CORAL: I'm on the toilet so much I might as well have it moved into the lounge so I can sit on it and watch the telly.

ALFA: Why don't you just go around with a bucket between your legs?

BEATY: I can't have children.

CORAL: I'm pregnant.

ALFA: What's that about being on your period, then?

CORAL: I was being nostalgic.

BEATY notices the lighting cue

BEATY: There's the lights – they're changing.

CORAL: *(A.D.)* We swiftly put away our toys as Alfa climbs into her dress.

(As self.) Beaty! Your embroidered knickers!

BEATY: What?

CORAL: You've left your appliquéd G-string on the stage!

BEATY: Thanks!

ALFA: I know it's only a brief interlude, but it gets briefer every night. I haven't had my soup, yet. I swear it's just so the crew can make last orders at the bar.

BEATY: Well, you have to get your priorities right…

The women take a moment to prepare for the next scene – Floods come on. The women move into stylised tableaux, establishing the change in dynamic for the 'parallel' play. ALFA continues as storyteller, the story she was rehearsing earlier. The others follow, as chorus,

Chorus

ALFA: Once, once there was an ancient city, high, set high among the olive terraces and the almond orchards – an ancient city of women and children, fatherless families – wandering the maze of narrow cobbled streets; happy to be together – grateful that, so far, they had escaped the fate of Troy.

CORAL: These women had lost their men to some fruitless battle over some unknown argument rooted centuries before…

BEATY: These women knew in which direction the world revolved and it was counter to them.

ALFA: They smelt the ash of a thousand burning bodies and sensed the military advance, watching the bruise of smoke deepen on the delicate flesh where the earth and the sky met.

CORAL: And these women knew the stories.

BEATY: Rape as a war tactic. Babies' heads split like conkers.

CORAL: And they knew what would happen.

Beat.

ALFA: So they made a decision, those women with their children in the ancient city high in the hills, amongst the flowering almond blossom and the olive terraces: They taught their children to dance

BEATY: Mamma's precious

CORAL: future joy

ALFA: they taught their children to dance and, clasping hands, they danced up along the city gates

BEATY: as the bruise deepened on the horizon

ALFA: they danced out, along the city's upper walls, past the lookout

CORAL: where the armour of the approaching army was clearly visible, glinting in the light

ALFA: beyond the cobbled roads, where the path stumbled into rock and mud they danced, up along the steep incline, hands clasped, tiny feet stamping the rhythm

BEATY: Mamma's precious

CORAL: future joy

ALFA: up towards the pinnacle

BEATY: as the soldiers grew closer

ALFA: where tiny feet faltered but were urged on, hands clasped, dancing, dragged

CORAL: Mothers' faces wet with tears

ALFA: feet dancing, on and on until there was no more land to dance on and their feet tripped on air and, hands clasped, dancing, dancing, they danced out and plummeted to their deaths.

(Beat.)
Floods off, the women still in chorus mode, but no longer 'on' – ALFA signs the dancers poised on the brink, then plummeting to their deaths.

BEATY: *(A.D.)* There is a pause in Alfa's signing hands – a hesitation before her fingers – the children and Mothers – descend. Descend.

CORAL: *(A.D.)* Beaty's eyes fill with tears.

BEATY: No they don't.

ALFA: *(A.D.)* She stares at Coral viciously.

BEATY: They don't.

CORAL: Okay.

BEATY: Say it.

CORAL: *(A.D.)* Beaty's eyes do not fill with tears.

(Beat.)

BEATY: *(As self.)* Thank you.

(She 'looks' out at the parallel drama happening before her.)

I hate this bit.

ALFA: Where are we?

BEATY: Killer-mummy bit – the aftermath…

(As pseudo-storyteller.) Some versions claim that heavenly creatures swooped and caught the fragile bodies before they smashed into the rocks below. Spared pain, delivered to safety, a happy ending, stopping our minds from imagining the broken, mangled bodies – bones splintering on impact, childrens' screams as they realise Mamma isn't to be trusted, after all –

CORAL: Versions that save us from the horrific contemplation of the Mothers' decisions and those last terrible moments….

BEATY: … Killing your own child.

ALFA: As you've probably gathered, this is not one of those versions.

BEATY: But we don't believe in the pretty stories, the 'being spared all that' – the lies. We believe in knowing the full picture so you can prepare yourself for the worst

CORAL: but also – why not? – hope for the future….?

BEATY: You know, you're so pathetic at times… completely pathetic.

CORAL: Beaty, you –

BEATY: Oh, shut up, will you? Just – shut up.

BLACKOUT

Two

*ALFA is knitting, BEATY reading an up-market gossip magazine and CORAL making changes with her costume. BEATY's magazine-related lines should be up-to-date, showbiz gossip taken from the week of performance. *Stars' names should be changed to the latest flavour of the month.*

ALFA: I sometimes think my entire life is spent behind screens:
At the hospital, here at the theatre, and when I'm sign-interpreting, I'm always kept apart, away from the action.

CORAL: In a performance, when it's happening, do you –

BEATY: – I think there's something really sinister about Brad Pitt* and Angelina Jolie.*

CORAL: What?!

ALFA: Even at the hospital I've a bit part. *(As nurse.)* 'Pop your clothes off and the doctor will be with you in a moment' – all the drama and interesting shenanigans happen the other side of the screen to me.

BEATY: *(Of magazine.)* I like her hair colour. D'you think it'd suit me?

CORAL: What?!

ALFA: But it's even worse here – I'm an actor – I should be full of action rather than the passive recounter of doom.

BEATY: *(Of magazine.)* Jesus, she's really put on weight.

CORAL: Beaty, d'you mind putting down the magazine and giving me a hand with the costume-change?

BEATY: I'm busy.

CORAL: Please?

ALFA: The done-to, that's me.

CORAL: Pretty please?

ALFA: I'm never the doer.

CORAL: Alfa?

BEATY: She's busy knitting.

CORAL: Well, piss off, the lot of you, then!

BEATY: Ooooh…madam…

ALFA: *(Noticing CORAL's physical huff.)* Is she getting a strop on?

BEATY: Yeah.

ALFA: She does that.

BEATY: Yes, she does do that.

ALFA: Get a strop on.

BEATY: I know.

ALFA: Terrible.

BEATY: Not enough sex

ALFA: or chocolate

BEATY: or both

ALFA/BEATY: at the same time.

ALFA: Oh – she didn't like that.

BEATY: No – she didn't like that.

ALFA: *(A.D.)* Alfa admires Coral's disapproving little pout.

CORAL: I haven't got a disapproving little pout.

ALFA: *(A.D.)* Coral's pinching facial expression tells otherwise.

CORAL: That's not fair. You're describing me all wrong.

BEATY: *(A.D.)* Her face shrivels with indignation, becoming mean, ugly and malignant like a tumour.

CORAL: Oh great, insult by audio-description.

BEATY: *(A.D.)* Her lips pucker; her nostrils flare self-righteously.

CORAL: They did not do that! I couldn't do that if I tried!

ALFA: *(A.D.)* Coral tries to be the indignant ingénue, but is unfortunately too old to play that part.

CORAL: You're not telling the truth!

ALFA: You're in a war play, dearie. Surely you know in a war play, the first casualty is truth?

(Pause.)

Remember that time we were appearing in *Metamorphosis* in Watford and there was a fire? *(As DSM.)* 'Mr Sun is in the building...' and they evacuated the theatre, but left us beetled-up on stage? She got stroppy then, as well.

CORAL: I wasn't a dung beetle. I was playing a black widow spider, stuck upside down in some kind of web.

ALFA: Yeah, I remember – that giant rope ladder from the Army and Navy stores. None of it adequately fire-proofed. We could have fried.

CORAL: Us and the wheelies abandoned in the front row. Just as well it was a false alarm.

ALFA: And after, when they realised they'd left us, that bloody theatre manager running round screaming:

CORAL: 'And this is why "handicaps" are a health and safety risk.'

BEATY: Prick.

ALFA: There was cause, then, to be judgemental, to get a strop on.
That was justified.

BEATY: *(Flicking through her magazine.)* Now Justin Bieber*...I wouldn't touch him with a bloody barge pole.

ALFA: I wouldn't touch anyone. I'm more a unicycle than a tandem these days, if you get my meaning. Unless you want a family, or you've met the love of your life – which I think is a myth – why bother? Life's complicated enough as it is.

Did you know that women over thirty in New York are more likely to develop cancer AND be a victim of violent crime than have a lasting monogamous relationship with a straight man?

BEATY: Did you know when you mix avocado and garlic and lemon juice, you get guacamole?

ALFA: Did you know the end of the world is nigh?

BEATY: Did you know some lipsticks are shiny because they put fish scales in them?

ALFA: Did you know urine is a sterile antiseptic?

CORAL: Did you know the most famous disabled woman is Helen bloody Keller?

BEATY: Is that her name? Helen Bloody-Keller? As in double-barrelled..

CORAL: But to people she's 'the Marvellous Helen Bloody-Keller, a sort of Superspas'.

ALFA: 'Disabled people are the heroes of our time.' Peter Brook said that.

CORAL: Heroes for whom?

ALFA: Exactly.

BEATY: Right! If you two are starting…

BEATY starts getting herself out of her dress

CORAL: Where are you going?

BEATY: For a bit of a breather and a change of altitude. I get a bit suffocated on the rarefied air you two breathe up here on the high ground.

ALFA: What?

BEATY: We're bloody performers, not an equal opportunities steering panel!! I'm tired of the disability politics.

CORAL: *(Quietly.)* Well, we all know why, don't we….?

BEATY: Excuse me?!

CORAL: Nothing!

BEATY: My only disability is society and other peoples' prejudices –

CORAL: Oh, well said.

BEATY glares at CORAL – a moment of tension – then she moves downstage.

ALFA: Where are you going?

BEATY: To have a look at the action.

ALFA: So where are we, then?

CORAL: Towards the end of Act Two: The fall of Troy and slaughter of the innocents.

ALFA: Oh, I like that bit…wait for me.

(A.D.) The extras – i.e. us – stare, with varying levels of involvement, at the dramatic scene going on before them.

They do so.

CORAL: In a performance, when it's happening, do you…

BEATY/ALFA: …Sssssh.

CORAL: *(A.D.)* Beaty and Alfa are enthralled, lip-syncing the actors, up-staging them, in the dark. *(As self.)* Like they do in this scene, every bloody night.

BEATY: I'd love to play Andromache. I could do it better than her. *(She refers to the (unseen) performer on stage.)*

(As Andromache.) I nursed for nothing.
In vain the labour pains and long sickness

ALFA: Oh, bless.

BEATY: *(As Andromache.)* I have no strength to save my children from execution,
Nor the children of other mothers

ALFA/BEATY: who are suffering no less than me.

CORAL: In a performance, when it's happening, do you –

ALFA/BEATY: Sssssh…

BEATY: I love this bit…

ALFA and BEATY create the illusion of watching an emotional scene in the unseen parallel play. This continues under the following text.

ALFA: They're going to kill her little boy…

(BSL only.) Beautiful.

ALFA makes another happy, heartfelt sigh, reacting to what's happening 'on-stage'.

CORAL: *(A.D.)* Coral's attention wanders.

ALFA: So poignant… I wish someone would let me do a scene like that.

ALFA/BEATY: Oh!

ALFA: *(As Andromache.)* Child, your fingers clutch my dress.
What use, to nestle like a young bird under

the mother's wings?
('Observing', as self.) …Fantastic…

ALFA/BEATY: *(As Andromache.)* I cannot help you.

BEATY: *(As Andromache.)* My voice is hoarse from shouting, but no one hears…

ALFA: They're stuffed. No power, no hope, just the boys marching in and…

BEATY: I can't look at this bit when they take the baby. Have they taken him yet? Have they taken her baby?

ALFA: Well, that's fate, when you're Hector's child… You've got to be sacrificed… They can't keep alive a dead hero's son…

BEATY: Bastards.

ALFA: They're just following orders.

BEATY: Killing off the line…

CORAL: *(A.D.)* Coral's attention continues to wander, further out into the auditorium.
(As self.) In a performance, when it's happening, do you –

ALFA/BEATY: Ssssh…

CORAL: *(A.D.)* Beaty and Alfa are engrossed. Eyes on stalks.

ALFA: They'll never see each other again…

BEATY: I can't… (look.)

CORAL: *(A.D.)* Their attention is pinned to the action like an Amazonian butterfly onto a dusty baize presentation board.

ALFA: *(Whispered, as direction to unseen players.)* Just… yes…hold…hold…

CORAL: *(A.D.)* Alfa, unseen, conducts the actors on stage.

ALFA: ...that's it…yeees….hooollld…hooollldd…

BEATY: ...two...three...

ALFA: and releeeaaassse....

ALFA/BEATY: There!

CORAL: *(A.D.)* Alfa and Beaty smile satisfied and strangely self-congratulatory at each other.

ALFA: That timing!

BEATY: That was really good.

ALFA: Her discipline!

BEATY: Well, eight years doing psychophysical work...

ALFA: Exactly! I mean...

CORAL: *(A.D.)* They nod. Reminiscent of those little toy dogs that were put in the back window of cars in the seventies.

They nod.

But not our car, because we couldn't afford a car.

ALFA: I love seeing good work. Makes it all worthwhile.

BEATY: They did that scene really well... Let's hope the rest of the show doesn't suffer because of it...

CORAL: In a performance, when it's happening, do you ever watch the audience watching the show?

ALFA: No.

CORAL: You just sit there and ignore what's going on in front of you!?

ALFA: Yes. D'you want a hand with your costume change?

CORAL: Please.

BEATY: *(A.D.)* The performers help each other out of their big flashy dresses, revealing yet another frock underneath.

CORAL: Is this a posh war, or what? Red silk dresses…

ALFA: Don't knock it. I'm hoping to keep mine, afterwards. The cushion covers I could get out of that…

CORAL: It doesn't feel right.

ALFA: What do you want? A horsehair shirt?

CORAL: I thought we'd be in khaki.

ALFA: We're the chorus of a war play, not Kate bloody Adie. And the costume designer did train with Jean-Paul Gaultier…

BEATY: We could have ended up with conical tits! Imagine: us lifted, separated and strategically aimed…

ALFA: I'd rather that than some worthy interpretation. The Furies or Fates. Or the bloody Graeae sisters, with an eye and tooth shared between them…

CORAL: And, god forbid, if we were them, we might be meaningful and have to be taken seriously – given some status instead of bit parts, in the shadows.

BEATY: What's bitten you?

ALFA: Oh don't complain to anyone about the dresses…

CORAL: …You're right, I see that now. If we were dressed in khaki, that might suggest reality and make the audience think about us and what we're saying rather than the quality and texture of what we're wearing on our backs… Don't look at me like that.

(A.D.) Pensive, calculating – their mouths shrewish, eyes narrowed. *(As self.)* It wasn't me acting along with the principles, ready to sell my soul for a decent part…It wasn't me lip-syncing Andromache…
Don't you get tired of being the decoration… the right-on extras stuck at the back whilst the real actors continue with the real play…?

ALFA: I'm tired of pretending I'm not Deaf and having to work out all my visual cues on my own.

CORAL: Well, I've had it with bath chairs. I'm not doing a period piece again.

ALFA: I'd love to be part of an all-signing chorus.

CORAL: And my agent…if he ever puts me up again for a casting for *'Aliens'*…

ALFA: Don't. Go. There.

BEATY: *(A.D.)* Beaty has been watching all this, silently, her teeth lightly catching on the ulcer growing on the inside of her mouth. *(As self.)* Well, if I get a job, it's completely down to my talent.

CORAL: Yeah, the talent to be the ticked box on an equal opportunities monitoring form. Don't be modest. That's how you got this job.

BEATY: My, aren't we bitter and twisted?

CORAL: Look, even when we're ideal for the part we don't get it.

BEATY: I know you would have been a brilliant Hedda Gabler and you were born to play Joan of Arc, but disappointments happen and you just have to –

CORAL: – You know what I mean…

BEATY: … No. Don't use excuses and don't include me in your resume of failure.

CORAL: Excuses!

BEATY: It's a tough business.

CORAL: Even when it's a disabled character, they give it to a walkie-talkie.

BEATY: No one said it would be easy.

ALFA: Cripping up. The 21st century's answer to blacking up.

BEATY: If you can't run with the big dogs, stay on the bloody porch.

BEATY turns her back on them. Several beats.

CORAL: Did you hear? They're casting a biopic of Tamara De Treaux.

ALFA: Tamara…?

CORAL: De Treaux. You know, the famous Hollywood actress who played ET.

BEATY: When?! I'd be perfect! I'd be absolutely…

CORAL: …Apparently they're going to cast Renee Zellweger* or Jennifer Lawrence* and then digitally shrink her down to size.

BEATY: What?!

CORAL: CGI – computer generated imagery. Haven't you seen Lord of the Rings?

ALFA: So maybe they could film you and then blow you up to size.

BEATY: I am to size, fuck face.

ALFA: You have such a problem with aggression.

BEATY: No – I have such a problem with you being a fuckwit.

BEATY makes up a sign to denote fuckwit

ALFA: No – it's FUCK. *(She demonstrates.)* You make a circle with your finger and thumb and then with the middle finger of your other hand, you penetrate the circle again and again. Fuckfuckfuckfuckfuckfuckfuckfuckfuck

Pause.

CORAL: Do you think we all end up just like our mothers? If we had kids, would we make the same mistakes?

ALFA: Where did that come from?

CORAL: Nowhere…just… *(To BEATY.)* In a performance, when it's happening, do you ever watch the audience watching the show?

BEATY: Yes. I make a mental note of who yawned and who forgot to switch off their mobile phone, then I have a contract taken out on them.

ALFA: The magic of theatre. Live performance as a collaborative act, the dynamic created by the relationship between the spectacle and the spectators. That's why no two performances are the same. It's symbiotic.

BEATY: Exactly. And if the audience don't respect that, they're asking for their legs to be broken…
(A.D.) We look out at the audience expectantly.

Several beats as they stare at the audience expectantly.

(A.D.) Slowly the expectation turns to boredom and disappointment. Only Coral remains staring.

CORAL: I watch them – the audience – their heads sleek in the dark – furtive – secretive, with their little habits, tics, inappropriate coughs, gaze. I watch them – but it's transgressive

– I'm to be stared at, not them. But I look and I want to ask who are you? Why are you here? What do you think of me? As you sit there in your rows in the dark, rubbing shoulders with strangers, looking, listening – what do you think of me? Am I just another performer? What am I? My Mother could never find the exact word for me – even though she's still searching.

(As mother.) 'What are you like Coral? I'll tell you what you're like: A disappointment. A let-down. And after all my sacrifices…'

(To audience as self.) I'm watching you.

Beat.

BEATY: We're on.

Chorus

CORAL: And as the battle commenced and the

BEATY: heat-seeking missiles

ALFA: arrows

BEATY: bayonettes

CORAL: stones found their mark and as the

ALFA: soldiers

CORAL: mercenaries

BEATY: widow-makers

CORAL: serial killers

ALFA: former-neighbours advanced

ALL: on both sides;

CORAL: and as the mortar

ALFA: shrapnel

BEATY: boiling oil

CORAL: poured down,

ALFA: we sat in the ruins and laughed:

ALL: Haven't we been here, before?

CORAL: And as the radio blared

ALFA: and the spider shuttled back and forth into the corner

BEATY: and the children were taught marching songs in the courtyard

ALFA: we signed their death warrants

CORAL: by not saying

ALL: no.

ALFA: Child – I should have taken your nursery pillow and suffocated you myself rather than leave you to bleed dry on no-man's-land.

BEATY: I should have crushed you in the womb – folded you back inside myself rather than let you die by suicide bomb in a crowded discotheque.

CORAL: Her hope is that he died, dancing

BEATY: Mama's precious

ALFA: future joy

BEATY: hands clasped, dancing, dancing.....

ALFA signs a version of the 'dance of death' as at the end of Scene One.

CORAL: *(A.D.)* Alfa's fingers dance, dancing, dance down the deaths...

The moment is slowed, completed. Floods go off. A beat.

CORAL: I'm pregnant.

(Beat.)

ALFA: *(To BEATY.)* She's pregnant.

BEATY: How?

CORAL: Immaculate conception second time round. How d'you think?

ALFA: She shagged somebody. A man. Shagged him.

CORAL: And this is doing my head in… This play is… help me.

BEATY: What?

CORAL: Help me by telling me.

BEATY: What d'you want me to say?

CORAL: That it'll be all right. That… that earth's an okay place to take a baby… That… I'd be a good mum… That…

BEATY: But we don't know that, do we?

CORAL: What?

BEATY: Any of it. We don't know any of it.

CORAL: But tell me.

BEATY: I can't answer that. I don't know.

CORAL: Please…

BEATY: You want me to lie?

(Beat.)

ALFA: *(A.D.)* Coral looks at Beaty, who doesn't speak. Alfa takes out her knitting.

BEATY: *(A.D.)* Beaty sets up her mirror, takes out her lipstick and prepares for the next scene.

They do as described.

CORAL: Please.

ALFA: *(A.D.)* A painful pause

(A painful pause.)

(As self.) How about the dad?

CORAL: Gone. I asked him to, it – it wasn't really working – and I'm happier alone.

BEATY: Why'd you get pregnant if you didn't want to get pregnant?

CORAL: It wasn't planned.

ALFA: Were you taken by force?

CORAL: No… It seemed a good idea at the time.

BEATY: I've a really nice recipe for sweet potatoes. You put them in olive oil and in the oven and when they come out, they're all really nice and soft.

ALFA: Is there a low fat version?

CORAL: It'd be irresponsible for me to have a baby I don't really want.

BEATY: Exactly. Story over. Move on.

CORAL: Are things always so black and white to you?

BEATY: Yes.

ALFA: *(To BEATY.)* You know – that lipstick really suits you.

BEATY: Oh, thanks.

CORAL: But it doesn't stop me from thinking about it.
It's real. It could happen.
I could have… I could…
If things were different, I'd have it. I'd like to look after it in a family– what's that stupid word? Nuclear? Nuclear family. Only I'd have mum, dad, baby and fucking personal assistant. I wouldn't do that, subjecting a baby to that. No privacy. All those people… passed around, one pair of stranger's hands to another. Not knowing whose arms are holding you.
Watching mummy be patronised, treated as an incompetent; some kind of Frankenstein with her new-born baby. I couldn't put a child through that. I couldn't. Never mind

everything else – how unsafe the world is… how suddenly filled with sharp edges and…

BEATY: Great. Decision made. End of conversation.

CORAL: No! I was still speaking, I was…

BEATY: Shit, or get off the pot.

CORAL: What?!

BEATY: You're going on and on and on. Make the decision. Or if you're going to whinge, be a bit more entertaining, would you?

CORAL: What's wrong with you?

BEATY: You wittering on about this frigging baby.

ALFA: It's not a baby. It's a collection of cells. A blood clot. Little more than a minor thrombosis and nothing you say will convince me otherwise.

(Beat.)

CORAL: Well, thank you, both.
This is probably the most important decision I'll ever make in my life. I thought you'd understand, help me think it through, but no. Who was I kidding? Just forget it. Just forget I ever said anything.

BEATY: Ooooh. Little Miss Tantrum…

CORAL: Conversation closed.

BEATY: Don't take it out on us that you're so crap with contraceptives.

CORAL: Dialogue finito.

BEATY: Wasn't us that put you up the duff off the rag and in the family way.

CORAL: Just leave it.

BEATY: Why?

CORAL: Just…

BEATY: Why?

CORAL: Because you wouldn't know a helpful, sympathetic thing to say if it jumped up and bit you in the arse. Because you don't understand.

BEATY: No?

CORAL: Because you're so lacking in the milk of human kindness, you've gone rancid. Because you haven't the slightest idea…

BEATY: *(Interrupting.)* I've had to make the same decision.

(Beat.)

I've had a child. But I've not been a mother. I've had a child. But it's not the same.

CORAL: Isn't it?

BEATY: It doesn't count. I had all the biology…the physical sensations – that new life moving under my hand…stirring inside…waking me in the night…

CORAL: But you haven't mothered?

BEATY: No.

ALFA: And it's not the same.

BEATY: *(To ALFA.)* And you'd know about that, would you?

ALFA: I know a sad woman when I see one.

BEATY: Know all about babies? About carrying them and giving birth?

ALFA: Ugly and sad. It's there, in your mouth.

CORAL: *(A.D.)* Alfa's hand shapes the air.

ALFA: I can see it. *(A.D.)* Sorrow. The lips pulling down, mouth sunken with its weight.

BEATY: I don't want to hear this.

ALFA: You can always tell who got rid of their baby.

BEATY: *(Overlapping.)* Enough, that's enough.

ALFA: In a room full of people, or walking down a crowded road, you can always tell…

BEATY: I'm not listening.

ALFA: It leaves its traces – an ugliness, a sorrow, a –

BEATY: I've stopped listening to you. Oi! Deafie!

She sticks two fingers up at ALFA.

CORAL: *(A.D.)* Beaty sticks two fingers up in a very un-Churchill like kind of way.

BEATY: Sign language everyone can understand.

ALFA: Only if you can see.

BEATY: Just leave it – shut the fuck up, okay?

ALFA: I hate being in the chorus with you. You're an ugly person, Beaty, did you know that?

BEATY: I'm ugly?

ALFA: I'm not talking appearance; I'm talking inside. Ugly ugly ugly

BEATY: Watch it...

ALFA: Ugly ugly ugly

BEATY: You're so ugly, your Mother didn't give birth to you. She shat you.

ALFA: You're so ugly, when you were born, the midwife slapped your mother.

BEATY: I'm so ugly, I couldn't be a fucking Mother. I gave her away – freely, by choice, voluntarily, after what's considered fair and balanced professional advice. I had the baby and she was taken away from me, because – guess what? – I'm a 'special person' who isn't going to be around on this planet for very long and that's not the best criteria for bringing up a baby. Is it? And because I'm a freaky damaged sick chick and because I have an interesting and increasingly rare genetic conjunction, and because I was led to believe I wouldn't see past 20, it's best to tie the tubes – no, better still – slice them – as we don't want the special egg meeting with the sperm again, do we? We don't want this freaky evolution to continue, do we? I mean 'special' is scary, expensive, a drain on limited welfare resources and you want to be a good citizen, don't you? You want to be responsible and caring, you want the best for yourself and your child, so be a good girl and sign along the dotted line, freely, willingly, of your own accord.

So I did.
And they took the baby and sterilised me.
And everything was my choice.

(Long pause.)

CORAL: I'm sorry.

BEATY: The last of my line.

CORAL: And the baby?

Beat.

What happened to the baby? Did the baby survive?

BEATY: Yes.

CORAL: Was the baby adopted? Beaty?
Was the baby adop – ?

BEATY: – By a nice non-disabled family with a life expectancy much longer than the biological mother's. And that's all I'm gonna say about it.

CORAL: But –?

BEATY: It's none of your fucking business.

CORAL: But we've just…

BEATY: …I work with you, you're not my best friend and just because we've both had a bun in the oven doesn't mean we're sisters under the skin.

CORAL: Beaty you just told me...

BEATY: We haven't shared anything significant, just an unfortunate coincidence.

CORAL: …but the baby, the…

BEATY: If you put a slice of brown bread with garlic and some parsley into the microwave for less than a minute, then eat it up quickly before it goes hard – you'll have a nice something for when you're in from work, feeling tired and wanting a snack. And the parsley's great as it gets rid of the garlic smell…

CORAL: Stop it! Just chitchat chit fucking chit chat.

BEATY: Don't you like chit chat?

CORAL: No, I don't fucking like chit chat and I don't like garlic on brown fucking sliced bread.

BEATY: What about ciabatta? Seeded bread rolls, rye bread? How about thinly sliced white bleached processed bread…?

CORAL: Don't you ever take anything seriously?

BEATY: No. Because life's too short…

She applauds.

So good old Coral…good on you, having a bun in the oven. A little loaf. Your yeasty high-riser. What kind is it, eh? Irish soda bread – was the daddy a paddy?….or petit pain – maybe he was French…

CORAL: Beaty…

BEATY: …Or a Scottish griddle cake….

ALFA: *(A.D.)* Beaty has gone off in a world of her own.

BEATY: ….maybe Italian Focaccia….

ALFA: *(A.D.)* Beaty lists all the bread she can remember.

BEATY: ...Well, there's always the American Wonder loaf;

ALFA: *(A.D.)* As she does so, Alfa rages in BSL – the story she wants to tell –

BEATY: ...sweet zucchini bread...

ALFA: – a terrible one, about women who had no choice...

ALFA signs her story using BSL or visual language, but with no voice, whilst BEATY very slowly lists the breads.

BEATY: Sour dough balls; baguette; Walnut pave; organic sundried tomato and basil plait; Hovis; Sunblest; Nimble; wholemeal bloomer; cholla; oaty tin; cheese and onion bread; panini; garlic and coriander naan; chapattis; pitta bread; poppyseed rolls; floury baps; warburtons; scofa; Irish boxty; poppadoms; French stick; wheatgerm;

The following is an English language précis of what ALFA will sign in performance, using BSL or visual language. It is reproduced here in this version solely for the purposes of the published text and in performance, even a captioned one, there should be no English translation.

(Another version of this speech occurs in Scene 3, with a translation into spoken English, using the syntax of the original signed speech.)

ALFA: *(No voice.)* A story from the war. A woman. This way the laboratories. This way the crematoriums. Many had not survived – those who were blind, or had polio, or – . She was Deaf. She survived. She was useful. Could work. She was 'allowed' to survive – but with one amendment. They sterilised all the men and women.

After...life went on. People worked, people died. She married, but had no children. People asked: why don't you have children? Why can't you have children? Are you sterile, then? Stupid? Why don't you have children? They were silent. They did not speak about it. The war was over – and she was silent – he was silent – waiting for the knock on the door, the butt of a revolver against the skull. She lived daily with fear of violence should she tell what happened to her in the camps. She was one of hundreds, perhaps thousands … subjects of former experiments, trapped behind their net curtains, caught in a binding agreement not to tell, never to tell. All stuck. All silent.

Our story.

(With sounding voice.) Schtum.

ALFA's signing of the story and BEATY's naming of bread come to an end. A pause. CORAL looks at ALFA expectantly.

ALFA: *(With sounding voice.)* I'm not going to voice-over for you so don't look at me expecting an interpretation.

CORAL: But…I…but…but you…

ALFA: It's not a secret language. It's in the public domain. I'm not going to cheapen my exquisite signing with your words.

CORAL: But…you…but…but…

ALFA: *(Signed only.)* Jawjawjawjaw, bloody talkies, always eating air.
(Sounding voice.) Learn it yourself.

(Several beats.)

The floods come on – BEATY moves downstage, caught in a spotlight for the parallel play.

BEATY: All men know children mean more than life.

Which is why they kill them.

BLACKOUT

Three

A huge wall of sound: loud music with explosions, sirens and gunfire beneath, many reverberations.

When the lights come up, the women are out of their silk dresses, wearing worn clothes. The sounds and vibrations continue intermittently throughout the start of the scene. The women do not react to them, except as a brief silence, then continuing with their speech/actions. The women are involved in small, slowed activities. They help each other remove their costumes. ALFA is finishing making the soup she was making, earlier. Later, she passes around bowls and they eat.

They speak a 'non-chorus' at the opening of the scene, i.e., they are no longer the chorus, although they still assume the form. They speak in their usual voices, everyday, tired, with no performance mode. Even the audio description (A.D.) is closer to their usual voices and lacks the presentation of before. There are no floods.

Non-chorus

ALFA: And as the trumpets

BEATY: wailing

CORAL: all-clear sounded, the women came forward to harvest their fallen fruit.
Fields ripe with a strange crop

ALFA: limbs

BEATY: torsos

ALFA: arms

CORAL: heads

ALL: plucked

CORAL: ready to be gathered.

BEATY: Here a hand relaxed, palm open, lying as it did so frequently in life.

CORAL: Here a body, soft, almost in repose

BEATY: faces twisted

CORAL: teeth bared

ALFA: eyes rolled back

ALL: dead.

CORAL: All dead.

ALFA: They claim them, the living, crawling across the rubble

BEATY: seeking the familiar known faces

ALFA: remembered hands

CORAL: half-forgotten birthmarks

BEATY: flesh that when new was bathed, kissed, patted dry, powdered

ALFA: sung over

BEATY: lullabyed

ALFA: Mama's precious

CORAL: future joy

BEATY: now rank

ALFA: sullied

BEATY: gone forever

ALL: Child. Child.

(Beat.)

CORAL: They've forgotten about us.

(Beat.)

ALFA: Soup?

CORAL: Yes, please.

ALFA: *(AD.)* Coral is peering from within the now bare metal structures.
(As self.) It's awfully quiet.
Can you see the other side of the screen?

BEATY: No.

ALFA: I hate being behind a screen. I seem to spend my life behind a screen. I –

CORAL: Is anyone else feeling the heat? Have they switched off the air conditioning?

ALFA: Soup?

BEATY: Yes.

CORAL: *(A.D.)* Coral loosens her clothing. She sees everybody's face is beaded with sweat.

ALFA: *(A.D.)* We eat.

Several beats as they eat.

CORAL: Once. Once there was a Trojan horse wheeled in through the gates of the city, with death hidden in its belly.
An intelligent betrayal. Violence contained. Death controlled.
Now it just falls from the sky. It has no boundaries. It's invisible. War without frontiers. Or states. Or…

ALFA: …Has anybody got any painkillers?

CORAL: identification. It's faceless.

BEATY: I can do you codeine, ibuprofen, benylin, night nurse or aspro.

ALFA: Nothing stronger?

BEATY: Quaaludes and cipro?

CORAL: We sit eating oven-ready dinners on our laps in front of the telly, the volume turned low, whilst food parcels are dropped in the middle of minefields.

ALFA: I can't remember that speech from the play.

CORAL: The food we eat is poisoned. There are more wars raging now than in previous centuries put together.

ALFA: Is she rehearsing a new scene?

CORAL: As the ice caps melt, the land will be submerged. The planet is dying. We inject it with cancers and yet we still procreate, we still continue the old dance, covering our eyes, feet stamping the rhythm, mama's precious, future joy.

BEATY: I think her hormones are fucking her over. Gone tired and emotional, have we? A bit weepy?

CORAL: Fuck. You.

BEATY: That Oestrogen's a right bastard. Just chill. Have some more nice soup and borrow my mobile, call your boyfriend and give him the good news.

CORAL: Don't Patronise Me.

(Beat.)

ALFA: It's really quiet.
(A.D.) Alfa stares out into the darkness before her.
Why can't we see out? Have they brought the fire curtain down? Has everybody been sent home?
It really has gone awfully quiet.

BEATY: And you'd be able to tell the difference?

CORAL: Don't start.

ALFA: Is it over?

(Beat.)

Did anyone hear the applause?

(Beat.)

Was everyone sent home?

(Beat.)

Didn't the audience come back after the third interval?

CORAL: It's an epic all right.

ALFA: I've no idea what Act I'm in.
Where am I? Where was I?

CORAL: Women. Children. Variations on a theme.

BEATY: Men.

CORAL: Yeah, men. Women. Children. War. Women being strong.

BEATY: Killing their babies. *(A.D.)* Alfa flinches.

ALFA: I don't think I like this play very much.

BEATY: So when did you have your abortion?

A shocked silence

ALFA: It was supposed to be the ideal perfect punctuation two people who love each other plus baby full stop baby made up from each other as though we could disassemble ourselves then reinvent two as three and it was perfect, right from the start we felt we were doing more than making love we really were making life and I knew even before the pregnancy test I could feel it like there was a fizzing in my blood a secret I shared with my tissues and bones the fleshy matter that made up me and the father moved in and we booked the registry office and I *(slower)* arranged for an amniocentesis test ....

(Beat.)

What destroyed us was trying to decide where to put the blame. These two making three...when the sums don't add up – when the calculations are faulty – when the perfect multiplication comes out wrong – who made the mistake? Whose was the rogue gene?
I couldn't do it. The effort – the work involved – the never-ending dedication that was required, having ... that ... child. I couldn't do it. Okay? I couldn't fucking do it.

And then I realised nobody needed to know. I could keep my political correctness and my disability awareness and my halo still shining. I could remain holier than thou and get rid of it, flush it away, throw the blood-clot in the bin. So I did. And I asked the father to return my keys, pack his toothbrush and go off and worship some other flawed goddess, because I didn't deserve love, I needed to be punished. And I'm still serving time.
So do you have a problem with that?

BEATY: *(A.D.)* She looks at me, then out towards the auditorium.

ALFA: Have they forgotten about us?
Have they all gone home?

CORAL: *(A.D.)* Alfa strings a line of fairy lights between the structures.

BEATY: *(A.D.)* Beaty takes Alfa's bag of knittiing and empties it of finished garments. She begins pegging the clothes on the line…tiny white matinee jackets, new born baby's vest, booties…

(Beat.)

They rounded up all the men and male children and brought them to the stadium. The grass now grows over them.

CORAL: They bombed the people in the bread queue, then shot those trying to comfort the dying.

BEATY: They killed all the boys a moment before their fathers, so the men could see their hopes destroyed.

CORAL: Yesterday, four pupils were killed at their desks at school.

BEATY: There was an explosion in the market place.
People lay scattered.
Blood flowered on a woman's face.

CORAL: And they rounded up all the disabled people and took them to the camps.

ALFA repeats a version of the BSL eugenics speech of scene 2, BEATY and CORAL vocalise in BSL syntax.

ALFA: Chimney smoke queue move forward fire ash dead.
Building operation experiment
queue
blind limp deaf take throw operation cut sterilise pain
you go work
war peace
survivors go go go
life progress
some work
some die
some meet join marriage
children phho
people forward prod children why not?
Children phho can't you? Don't want?
Stupid? Children phho
children children children
prod prod prod prod.
Schtum.
Memory past war nerves door soliders
bang bang door open – gun
– you – tell – never –
schtum.
Alone? No. Many. House house house
person person person behind curtains look
stuck think war speak release? No.
Schtum
Stuck stuck stuck.
All schtum.

(Pause.)

BEATY: Have the baby.
Have the bloody baby.

(Beat.)

To make up for those we've lost.

CORAL: Oh yeah, right – let's all go out and have babies as some response to the holocaust. Or if not that atrocity, some other war; there's plenty to choose from.

BEATY: You talk such bullshit.

CORAL: No. This isn't a political theory, this is my life and I'm not convinced I want someone else to go through this.

ALFA: Go through – ?

CORAL: This. This life.

Several beats. The women reflect.

They go into performance chorus mode – no floods – this is their own version.

ALFA: So they made a decision, those women with their phantom children

BEATY: These women who knew in which direction the world revolved: counter to them.

ALFA: They smelt the ash of a thousand burning bodies, watching the bruise deepen on the delicate flesh where the earth and the sky met.

CORAL: And these women knew the stories and they knew what would happen

ALFA: so they taught their children to dance

BEATY: Mamma's precious

CORAL: future joy

ALFA: They taught their children to dance and, clasping hands, they danced up along the city gates

BEATY: as the bruise deepened on the horizon

ALFA: they danced out, along the city's upper walls, past the lookout

BEATY: mother's faces wet with tears

ALFA: beyond the cobbled roads, where the path stumbled into rock and mud they danced, up along the steep incline,

BEATY: hands clasped, tiny feet stamping the rhythm

ALFA: Mamma's precious

CORAL: future joy

They stop. A beat.

ALFA: *(To CORAL.)* Did you know you can make oranges less messy to eat by putting them in the freezer for half an hour before peeling them?

CORAL: Just fucking get on with it…

ALFA: With…?

(Pause.)

BEATY: *(A.D.)* They are silent.
They do not move.

(Beat.)

CORAL: I think I'm bleeding.

Immediate blackout.

End of play.

The Almond and the Seahorse

Reviews from the European premiere, February 08, Sherman Cymru Theatre

'Unmissable drama… Throughout Kaite O'Reilly's tremendous new play … extraordinary scenarios are tenderly drawn and powerfully realised…'

★★★★★ *The Guardian*

'A powerful drama, beautifully written…Compelling and emotionally charged'

The British Theatre Guide

'Kaite O'Reilly's powerful new play…impressively researched…Graveyard humour, poetic flights of fancy…superb…'

The Stage

'Copies of Kaite O'Reilly's play are available for sale… and I highly recommend buying a copy… this intelligent work…is full of observations on the nature of life, of relationships, of change, of ageing, which transcend the specific situation… this is a reflection on the depth of the content of the play which also has flashes of brilliance. A fascinating work, totally engaging…'

★★★★ *Western Mail*

'…Wonderful…a masterly and captivating performance…writing with such sensitive beauty and delicate understanding….what real theatre is all about.'

Michael Kelligan, *Theatre-Wales*

'…it is the beautifully drawn characters that makes this play so engaging. A strength of O'Reilly's writing is her ability to create complete, rounded, in depth characters that an audience can care about… .this brilliant play… bring[s] Disability Arts into a mainstream arena.'

Disability Arts Online

The Almond and The Seahorse was the launch production of Sherman Cymru Theatre, Cardiff, on 29 February 2008.

Cast

SARAH	Nia Gwynne
JOE	Celyn Jones
GWENNAN	Olwen Rees
TOM	Ian Saynor
DR IFE FALMER	Mojisola Adebayo

Gwennan is bilingual, speaking Welsh and English. I have used the Welsh language in this text from the original production, with the translation in English as footnotes. With thanks to Olwen Rees and Carri Munn for assistance with translations.

In other productions, Welsh has been replaced by 'mother tongue' languages appropriate to location and context (eg Irish Gaelic and English; Turkish and German).

Research Notes

Over the past four decades the amount of people surviving Traumatic Brain Injury (TBI) has increased so dramatically, on both sides of the Atlantic, it is called by TBI charities 'a silent epidemic'. Headway, the UK charity, estimates that in the 1970s 90% of all severe head-injured patients died; now, owing to medical and technological developments, the majority survive. These people are often cared for in the home. Road accidents account for 40-50% of all injuries; domestic and industrial accidents for 20-30%, sports and recreational injuries 10-15%; assaults (including war) account for 10%.

In the USA there have been more fatalities from head injury over the past twelve years than in all the wars in which the USA has ever fought. In the USA over 2% of the population live with a disability as a result of a brain injury. There are two million new cases a year of people with traumatic, moderate or mild head injury.

(Source: Head Injury, A Practical Guide, by Trevor Powell.)

DIFFERENT TYPES OF MEMORY:

Our memory systems work initially by taking in information through our senses, which goes into the information or sensory memory, which is held only for a few seconds. This information is then sent to the short-term memory, where it is held for a short period and then either rejected (erased) or passed on to a long-term store. Once in long-term store, it is relatively safe and includes personal experience memories, memories of all the knowledge and information we have learnt, plus procedure memory items (playing an instrument, riding a bike). However, depending on the form of injury, these too can be damaged or elements deleted.

Neuroscientist Oliver Sacks claims there are all sorts of memory: autobiographical; semantic; implicit; explicit; episodic; procedural; emotional; 'body' memory and musical memory, amongst others. See *The Man Who Mistook his Wife for a Hat* or *Musicophilia.*

Other useful resources: the case studies of neuropsychologist Paul Broks; Deborah Wearing's *Forever Today;* Cathy Crimmins' *Where is the Mango Princess? A Journey Back from Brain Injury*, information booklets from the UK charity Headway.

Characters

SARAH

is an archaeologist in her early thirties. She is married to Joe.

JOE

is the same age as Sarah and a former-plumber. Owing to a brain tumour, he has a reduced short-term memory and so is unable to lay down new memories.

TOM

is in his fifties. He has been full-time carer to his wife, Gwennan, for the past two decades.

GWENNAN

is in her fifties, formerly a music teacher, a cellist. Gwennan is a traumatic brain injury survivor, following a car crash which devastated her memory, making it stop prior to the point of impact. A Welsh speaker, she often delivers speeches bilingually.

DR IFE FALMER

is in her thirties, an ambitious neuropsychologist with experience of memory loss within her own family.

Gwennan and Joe are not victims, but survivors.

The action takes place in a variety of locations: Sarah and Joe's flat; the rooms, corridors and grounds of the respite centre (a residential/day clinic for those surviving TBI). The set is fluid and non-naturalistic.

Dr Falmer's notes are projected, visible to the audience.

Music: Bach's Cello Suite No.3 in C major. Sarabande.

This play is dedicated to Phillip Zarrilli and all the survivors.

1

Montage. TOM, SARAH, GWENNAN and JOE in separate areas, individual focus out, faces tightly lit, as if in a sea of darkness.

The distant sound of the sea.

TOM: It's a kind of dying.

SARAH: Could you help? It's my partner, Joe, he's missing.

GWENNAN: There was once a girl…

SARAH: I don't mean physically, I mean…

JOE: It's not safe.

SARAH: …there's a part of Joe that's gone missing and since then, it's a dead zone.

JOE: In the water, a man…drowning…

SARAH: His universe makes no sense. There's no continuity, no cause and effect, no logic.

GWENNAN: I know they're watching.

TOM: I'm not sure she even recognises me anymore.

SARAH: We're unmoored –

JOE: In the water – drowning, drowned –

SARAH: – just – drifting.

JOE: There's a man there's a man and he's in the water and he's…

SARAH: You have to live with someone who's lost their memory to realise *that* is what makes our lives.

GWENNAN: An age spot – there, on my hand.

SARAH: Memory.

JOE: …adrift.

TOM: It's not what you could call *a life.*

In her office at the respite centre, DR FALMER types – it appears projected onto the stage, visible to audience:

DR F/TYPE: Put your brain through a windscreen at 40 miles an hour and life becomes a lottery. You may remember things – or you may not.

Montage ends, but SARAH continues.

JOE and SARAH's flat, late at night. As she speaks, he enters the scene.

SARAH: Memory. That's the anchor – without, you're nowhere, just – we have to get it back. So if you could help… If you could find it and return it…if you…please…please…

JOE: Sarah?

What are you doing in here in the dark?

SARAH: Nothing. I was…

JOE: It's two in the morning. Come back to bed.

SARAH: Just a minute.

JOE: Sarah?

SARAH: – I know, Joe. I –

She embraces him suddenly; they hold each other tightly for a moment.

JOE: Come to bed.

End of sequence

Elsewhere, knocking, as on a locked door. TOM stands.

TOM: Gwen? Open the door, please?

Could you – would you let me in, please?

A striking cello chord. Continues into:

2

Respite centre. GWENNAN in 'the garden', a place of imagination. She speaks bilingually, using English and Cymraeg (Welsh).

GWENNAN: There once was a girl, a curious, adventurous, disobedient girl… She wandered where she was told not to, befriending the folk who took her down underground… They washed her hair although it wasn't dirty, gave her food which she took although she wasn't hungry and they led her in such dances – *roeddan nhw'n chwarae'r fath gemau efo hi.*[1] And she was happy and she lived with them, even fell in love with them and it was so restful, full of ease – *fel cwsg hir rhyfeddol.*[2] And then one day word came that the people from above ground wanted her back. They said they loved her and wanted her home. She had been stolen – *yn cael ei chadw'n garcharwr*[3] – her parents were dying, her beloved pining, they were suffering without her presence. She didn't want to go. *Nac oedd.*[4] They wouldn't accept she had chosen and so they attacked, smashing through the walls, leaving a pile of rubble as chambers collapsed. They were fearless and exacting in their executions but gentle with her, asking why would she want to live in the gloom, *yn y gwyll,*[5] in the whispered half silence? We have saved her, they told each other, liberated her from being buried alive. And they were gentle with her as they tore her into their sun and she blinked, dazzled by their light, and they said this is your world and she cried at the ugliness and they said this is your

1 That's the kind of games they played with her.
2 Like a long, wonderful sleep.
3 Imprisoned.
4 No, not at all.
5 In the gloom..

bridegroom, he has been waiting for you, caring for your parents, husbanding your home, now be a woman. And she gasped as she saw the grown man, the nearly old man, saying but I'm only a girl, can't you see? *Dim ond merch ydw i.*[6]

Knocking is heard. GWENNAN stops and sits quietly, staring ahead.

3

TOM, still on the other side of a locked door, waits. It becomes clear that it is GWENNAN's door within the respite centre.

TOM: I'm still here.

Gwennan? It's me. Tom. Your husband, Tom. Thomas. Thomas Williams. Thomas Lloyd Williams, from the Eisteddfod[7]. It had come to our town and I went to have a look. Mooching around, nothing else to do. Didn't belong there. Not a Welsh speaker, see. They didn't go in for that, or music or recitation in the dump I went to. Because that's what it was: a dump, it wasn't education, or not so you'd notice. Perhaps it was tough education like there's tough love, you know, being taught things from the school of hard knocks? Well I've certainly learnt, love. Whatever lesson I was supposed to learn, I have it now by heart.

DR FALMER approaches.

So I was mouthing off in English on the Maes,[8] chip on my shoulder a yard wide, and you said shame! Shame for using Saesneg[9] on the sacred bloody field and

6 I'm only a girl.
7 Welsh language cultural festival. Other productions have replaced this with the name of a festival, venue, or event appropriate to the second language.
8 Field, site of festival.
9 English.

I was stumped. Smitten, more like. And I looked at you and your cello case and said can I carry that for you? *(To DOCTOR.)* In a minute. *(To GWENNAN.)* And the next thing I was in a pavilion, and you were playing and I'd never heard anything so beautiful, before. They didn't go in for Bach where I came from. And you were awarded first place, of course, so I suggested taking you out to celebrate and *(To DOCTOR.)* One minute. *(To GWENNAN.)* And get this, and get this Gwennie – you said yes! Yes, to me, the dreamy no-hoper from the local tech' and an English speaker to boot. Couldn't believe it! Couldn't bloody believe it. Nineteen years of age and thought I'd won the bloody lottery.

DR FALMER: Perhaps she's best left for the night?

TOM: So I took you to some movie – action-packed, boys' stuff, guns and hormones, I can't remember its name now, didn't even watch it, just sat there in the dark watching the light from the screen flicker on your face.

DR FALMER: Mr… *(Checks clipboard.)* Williams?

TOM: And that was it. Simple as that. Heart on the sleeve, ring on the finger, till death us do part. The end.
So, Gwennan, Gwennie…So, now that we're reacquainted, will you open the door and let me in, please?

Beat.

Gwen?

Beat.

I'm not going until I see you, love.

DR FALMER: I'm not sure she can hear you.

TOM: Oh, she can. She can hear, she can hear me all right, can't you, love? She knows me. She knows my voice.
Don't you, Gwennie?

DR FALMER: I think I'm going to have to insist –

TOM: – I only want to say goodnight. Just goodnight, doctor.

DR FALMER: There are other people trying to sleep so I really think we should –

TOM: – Gwen? We're disturbing the other patients. Could you open the door so I could say goodnight?

DR FALMER: I think that perhaps –

TOM: – Please. It's me. Open the door?

DR FALMER: This isn't helping either of you. Can I suggest –

TOM: – She knows my voice, usually she responds to my voice – normally she –

DR FALMER: – I really think you should get yourself home now, have a rest.

TOM: What's happened?

DR FALMER: It's late. You need to get some sleep.

TOM: There's a change…

DR FALMER: Things will look better in the morning.

TOM: Tell me: do all doctors have a bag of stock phrases that they dole out, like amphetamines, at the first sign of distress? Because if there is anything being handed out, I'd prefer a real pill. I'm the walking bloody wounded right here, in front of you. Can't you give me something stronger for the pain than clichés?

DR FALMER: I think it's time to leave.

TOM: I'm shaking.

DR FALMER: I'm going to have to call security unless you go, now.
I mean it.

TOM: You didn't see me.

DR FALMER: I'm sorry.

TOM: I wasn't even here.

He turns and walks away. DR FALMER watches him go, then the focus shifts and she begins a public talk:

4

DR FALMER is delivering a popular science lecture on neuropsychology.

DR FALMER: Put your brain through a windscreen at 40 miles an hour, or let it fall fifteen feet down a ladder and life becomes a lottery. You may remember things or you may not – like the theme tune of *The Magic Roundabout*, the taste and sensations of your first kiss, the insult your sister said and then forgot but which plagues you some mornings at 2.30 and has ever since you were twenty… It's remarkable what that kilo and a half blob at the top of your neck files away. Following traumatic brain injury – TBI – suddenly you might not recognise your mother, or recall who was in the room with you two minutes ago. You might decide the name for table is 'antelope', you might not speak at all. You might never come round from that coma. Or you might come round aggressive and abusive, speaking only in Latin or humming the tune of *The Magic Roundabout* again and again and again. In some rare cases you may have been improved.

The dynamic shifts from delivering a talk to her sitting at her desk and making notes – some words, again, visible to the audience.

But one thing's for sure, your old self – the *premorbid* self – will have ended and the New You will have come into being – the same person but with new frontal lobes and therefore, potentially, a new personality to match.

5

SARAH and JOE's. SARAH is finishing a phone call. JOE is eating pizza from a take-away cardboard box. At times he teases her, tempting her with a slice, which he then eats himself.

SARAH: *(On phone.)* Really? The pauper's casket? That's very commendable, Mother, very green and ecological and…I just want to be sure that's what you want to meet eternity in… Well, compared to some of the Viking longboat tombs, or Neolithic burial mounds, the pyramids, it's pretty low tech, it's… I can't help comparing, I've a professional interest…I…fine, it's your funeral…I'm just a little concerned. It's not so long since Dad – okay! Fine…Look, Mam, I have to go – Joe's just cooked dinner… Of course he can! He's surprisingly good in the kitchen, actually… That nouveau gourmet Cordon Bleu stuff, yeah…Oh come on, he's not completely useless!

JOE: Thanks.

SARAH: In fact, he's doing Horseman Riding By tonight. Roasted quail stuffed with anchovy, wrapped in pork and – yeah… it'll get cold – yes – yes – love you too, bye!!

She hangs up the phone.

JOE: Horseman…?

SARAH: Don't even ask. It's only to blind her with bollocks – beat her into submission with recipes and ingredients she never knew existed. My mother thinks anchovy is a root vegetable and quail's one of those funny foreign spices that repeats and irritates her hiatus hernia...

She takes a slice of pizza, JOE goes to put the box down.

SARAH: Don't put the greasy pizza box there!

JOE: Okay, lady... Put the gun down...

SARAH: Sorry... Fall-out from a rather stressful phone call: She's been talking to undertakers.

JOE: Who has?

SARAH: My mother.

JOE: Yeah?

SARAH: She's been investigating funeral directors.

JOE: Does she know something we don't?

SARAH: She claims not. She said seeing as she wants to be cremated, it's a waste, all that good oak or mahogany, just to be burned – and she should know...

JOE/SARAH: ...her father was a cabinet-maker –

SARAH: – only the good oak or mahogany isn't really burned. They have false bottoms. It's a scam. The coffin slides into the incinerator – the false bottom gives way – and only the body falls into the furnace.

JOE: Bloody hell.

SARAH: And then the undertaker sells the same box to another inconsolable mourner – hoiks up the price, takes advantage of their grief. She says I'll be devastated by guilt for not appreciating her when she was alive, I'll be susceptible to the funereal sales pitch, so she's choosing her own casket, now. The pauper's coffin. I tried talking her out of it, but she said she doesn't care if it's a banana box, a tea chest, or something made of recycled cardboard so long as it gets her to the crematorium, covered. And there's to be no viewing of the body. Or scary make-up – that disco Seventies blue eyeshadow is so not a good look on a seventy-year-old corpse. She says it's healthy to have an interest.

JOE: In what?

SARAH: In how we shuffle off this mortal coil.

JOE: What brought that on?

SARAH: I don't know – maybe something in the paper, or… You know what my mother's like.

JOE: A small, squat, dumpy woman, five one, packing too much weight for one so '*petite*', hair dyed vaguely honey-blonde and a blinder of a smile reminiscent of yours.

SARAH: Very good, but I wasn't being literal.

JOE: You're looking very tired.

SARAH: That's because I am.

JOE: I hope you're not coming down with anything.

SARAH: No – it's alcohol poisoning and lack of sleep. I had my work do the other night – Jonesie's retirement gig.

JOE: He's retiring!?

SARAH: Put out to grass.

JOE: But Jonesie's one of the exhibits – a prime example of Unevolved Twentieth Century Welsh Man –

SARAH: – A distant relative of Pete Marsh, only preserved in alcohol rather than bog land. Killer of a party.

JOE: When?

SARAH: The other night.

JOE: So why wasn't I invited?

SARAH: Are you an archaeologist?

JOE: No.

SARAH: Could you hold your own in a conversation about the burials at Cave 5, the Klaises River mouth, Southern Africa, from about two thousand years ago? Or the Mesolithic burials at Vedbaek?

JOE: No.

SARAH: Well then. If you can't make small talk about the funeral rites of our predecessors over the canapés, you're not invited.
Ping. The light's just come on.

JOE: What?

SARAH: My mother and undertakers… It's my profession… She's frightened I'll decorate her with shell beads and antlers, bless her with red ochre, then bury her in the garden lying on a bearskin.

JOE: Not in Bethseda, you won't.

SARAH: Exactly.

JOE: You're looking very tired.

SARAH: You said.

JOE: Are you feeling okay?

SARAH: Nothing an early night won't cure.

JOE: So where shall we go for dinner?

SARAH: We've just had pizza…

JOE: I'm hungry. Are you sure we've eaten?

SARAH: There's the box.

JOE: But I'm starving. I haven't had anything to eat all day.

SARAH: You never stop eating! You're putting on weight and I hate going out with you; you start grinning and swearing, making those weird jokes, talking to strangers –

JOE: – Oh, that's lovely, that is. 'Don't smile, stop being friendly, don't connect, people may think there's something wrong with you.'

SARAH: But there is, Joe. You're disinhibited.

JOE: Great. Let's go to bed, then.

There is a moment between them, then, from nowhere:

So how many grandkids are we going to have?

SARAH: Grandkids?

JOE: Yeah. How many are we going to have?

SARAH: I don't know…

JOE: Three? A dozen? A pathetic, measly one?

SARAH: We haven't even talked about having children, so –

JOE: – It's a simple enough question! How many grandchildren are we going to have?

SARAH: I don't know.

JOE: Tell me.

SARAH: I can't answer, I –

JOE: – Please.

SARAH: Joe, I can't –

JOE: – How many grandchildren –

SARAH: – I can't answer that!

JOE: How many –

SARAH: – Seven. Three girls and four boys. They're called Rohid, Gusippie, Padraig, Fidel, Talullah, Sita and Finervere.
Happy now?

JOE: Why aren't there any Welsh names?

SARAH: Because we have eclectic and unusual children in law. Indian, Mexican, Irish and Cuban. Our offspring have travelled a lot and are prone to falling in love with unsuitable people in far-flung locations. One's an oceanographer and another sells fancy knickers through the internet. Another used to be a boy until she had a sex change and although she's still not sure if she's Arthur or Martha, she's destined to be the first transsexual in outer space. She's training now at Cape Canaveral. She's American. There's many, we have many children, of all shapes, sizes, denominations, sexual preferences and races. In fact, they're all shape-shifters, moving in and out of the possibilities, which are endless and unfathomable.

JOE: There's no need to take the piss. It was a perfectly reasonable question. Are you feeling okay?

SARAH: I'm fine.

JOE: You look really tired. Are you coming down with something?

SARAH: No.

JOE: You should take a few days off. Is Jonesie working you too hard?

SARAH: He left.

JOE: When?

SARAH: Last week.

JOE: No! Really?

SARAH: We just had his leaving do.

JOE: You kept that quiet. Jonesie's an institution. No – Jonesie's a fossil. He's always been there.

SARAH: He retired.

JOE: Who?

SARAH: Bryn Jones. At work.

JOE: Jonesie?

SARAH: Yes. He retired. Bryn Jones, at the university where I work, he retired.

JOE: Good luck to him. And I'm not surprised, if he worked half as hard as you do. You're very pale. Bags under your eyes. Hope you're not coming down with something. I'm going to have a word with that Jonesie.

SARAH: You know, I'm absolutely starving, aren't you?

JOE: He's one of those who'll be found dead curled up under his desk. He'll never retire.

SARAH: *(Overlapping.)* What d'you fancy for dinner? Pizza? Indian?

JOE: It really pisses me off he then inflicts his Protestant work ethic onto everyone else!

SARAH: Joe?

JOE: Look at you! You're getting old before your time.

SARAH: We could try and catch last orders for bar food at The Conwy.

JOE: I swear I can actually see you ageing.

SARAH: D'you fancy that? Or Chinese, maybe?

JOE: Are you feeling okay? You look pretty rough.

SARAH: *(Overlapping, very fast.)* I'm fine. I'm not ill – just getting older. I'm not ill; I'm getting older. I'm getting older, I'm not ill, I'm getting older, I'm getting older.

JOE: You *are* looking older.

SARAH: *(Normal speed.)* That's because I am. Older. I'm older than you remember, Joe.

JOE: From last night? How can you be older than from last night?

6

GWENNAN and DR FALMER in the respite centre.

GWENNAN: I don't think I can do this.
I said I don't think I can do this.

DR FALMER: You can. You always do. You always find a way. In your own time.

GWENNAN: 'In my own *time*...?! In my own...'

GWENNAN notices her hand – looks at it as though it were someone else's.

I've the beginnings of a liver spot. Age. There, on my hand. Never used to be there. Wasn't there yesterday. Nor the lines on my face. Smooth. That's how it was when I last looked. Ripened. Full. Now I'm like an apple that's been in the fruit bowl too long. Withered, drying out–
Are they all dead? Because if they are I'd like to know, now. None of this water torture, telling me drip by drip. I'd like to know now, in one big tidal wave so it's over and done with and there's no worries about what else has happened, what else you're keeping back from me until I'm stronger. For I'll never be stronger. This is the strongest I'll ever be. Here, now. So go on: tell me.

DR FALMER: If that's what you want, Gwennan.

GWENNAN: Just give me a minute.

Beat, she looks at her hand.

Brychni – o phan roedd yr angylion yn ail – addurno'r nefoedd a doeddan nhw ddim yn rhy ofalus efo'r brwsh.
(She translates.) Freckles – from when the

angels were redecorating heaven and they weren't too careful with the brush… Stupid things you tell children – but they ask so many questions – I did – my mother would tell me anything just to have ten minutes peace.
'Why are freckles, Mam?' Why, mind, not what.
'Pam bod brychni?'
'Roedda ti yn y ffordd pan roedda nhw'n ail – addurno'r nefoedd a ges ti dy dasgu efo brwsh yr angel diog.'

She repeats, translating for DR FALMER.

'Why are freckles?'
'You were in the way when they were redecorating heaven and you got splattered with the lazy angel's paintbrush.'
The marks wouldn't come off after I was born, as you can't get celestial turpentine on earth.
The nonsense you fill children's heads with.
It's criminal.
It should be truth we're told, not lies. We should be prepared from an early age, not have our heads filled with stories of hope and fairness and happy ever afters, because life's not like that. It's cruel. It's….

She looks at her hand.

So when exactly do angel freckles become hated liver spots? My mother would know.
My mother would.
But she's dead, you say?

DR FALMER: I'm sorry.

GWENNAN: Mam.
Dead.
Was it a long time ago?

DR FALMER: Four years.

GWENNAN: Four…?
Did I go? To the funeral, I mean.

DR FALMER: You were too upset.

GWENNAN: Was it a good turn out?

DR FALMER: I've a description here that your husband –

GWENNAN: – Just a simple yes or no. I don't want to read, I don't want

DR FALMER: – Yes. It was a good turn out. The chapel was full, the whole –

GWENNAN: – That's enough, now. That'll do.

Beat.

Thank you.

Beat.

A full chapel. She would have liked that. Expected it.

Beat.

And Thomas? My husband? Is he still alive?

DR FALMER: Yes.

GWENNAN: Good.

DR FALMER: You live with him.

GWENNAN: Oh!

DR FALMER: Not all the time. You're often here in respite.

GWENNAN: Respite.

DR FALMER: To give you both a break.

GWENNAN: Right.
Right.

DR FALMER: Just try and relax; concentrate on your breathing for me please Gwennan. Would it help if I put on some classical music? It can be very soothing – and I see from your notes you used to play the cello.

GWENNAN: *Used* to?

DR FALMER: You haven't played for some time, now. You still can – you haven't lost the facility. You still are able to play the cello – in fact it would be very beneficial – you just don't – or haven't.

GWENNAN: I –

DR FALMER: Focus on your breathing now, please. That's it. *(They breathe quietly together.)* You'll be fine.

They breathe together. Some time passes.

Good.

GWENNAN: So how long have I been out?

DR FALMER: Out?

GWENNAN: In the coma. How long was I in the coma for?

DR FALMER: It wasn't a coma.

GWENNAN: Asleep, then. How long have I been asleep?

DR FALMER: This may be difficult to understand, but you've been conscious all the time.

GWENNAN: But – then how –?

DR FALMER: There was a car crash and you sustained a severe head injury and –

GWENNAN: – When?

DR FALMER: Some time ago, now –

GWENNAN: – When?!

7

Focus shifts to TOM. He tells the story and partway through DR FALMER becomes visible, in her office, listening intently and making notes. Although initially in separate locations, there should be a sense of connection – that he is telling her this in a session – and by the end of the scene, he is in her office.

TOM: It's like a kind of dying. Every morning.
Every single morning, with no let-up, no break in routine.
She stirs, usually because of the sun shining in through the bedroom window. Gwennan stirs and, not yet fully awake, she slips from the bed and across to the bathroom. She walks with her eyes half closed; she could do it in her sleep. She pushes the bathroom door; it creaks. I hear the toilet flush, then the tap come on and then, after she's splashed her face with cold water and started to straighten up before the mirror, there's this tiniest pause before her scream.
That's the moment; the moment she sees herself, is confronted by what's happened. And there's a pause as she struggles to understand what she sees; she thinks it's the water in her eyes, or blurry sight from a deep sleep – but no. Her eyes refocus and there she is – twenty years older overnight.
Every morning. She has to go through this every morning. And then it's my job to calm her and explain – but she shrinks away from me, fear in her eyes – I *look* like her husband, but there's greying hair and lines on my face – she's repulsed. She finds my ageing repulsive. I'm not sure she even recognises me anymore…
For a while I tried taking down the mirrors.
I thought, naively, stupidly, it was kinder for her to continue thinking it was the late eighties and she was still newly married,

with a baby on the way. So I took down the mirrors, or turned them round to face the wall, but she was still shocked at how I'd changed – my apparent rapid ageing. There's not a lot I can do about that. Time catches up with us all, eventually. We can't hide getting older, just like I couldn't hide Gwennan's reflection from her in the lights and fitting section of B&Q when we were out shopping one Saturday morning.
So the bathroom mirror went back up. Better to get it over first thing.
So that's what we do every morning. Every single morning, except when she's in respite. I've almost got used to it. But not Gwennan. For her, it's the first time. Every morning is the first time she discovers her life's been stolen – how else can I describe it? She's not twenty-nine. She's not carrying our baby. Over twenty years have gone by and she has no recollection.
It's a kind of dying – her future's been wiped out but she's still alive. And there's nothing to be done. Nothing we can do.

TOM leaves DR FALMER's office. He and SARAH look at each other as they pass.

DR FALMER types – it is projected:

DR F/TYPE: Nothing to be done.
Nothing we can do (?)

8

Dr Falmer's office. DR FALMER is instructing SARAH in the use of recording equipment as memory aid.

Simultaneously, the focus comes onto JOE at home. There is a split stage – SARAH and DR FALMER in the centre and JOE at home, where there is a chair, the landline phone and a table, all placed separately, all with ashtrays.

DR FALMER glances through SARAH's notes, returns them to her, pats her shoulder encouragingly and leaves.

SARAH prepares to make a recording. In the flat, JOE is about to light a cigarette when he sees a tape recorder with a notice: JOE: SWITCH ME ON. He half laughs and switches it on. SARAH reads her notes live; they are the recording JOE is listening to in the flat.

SARAH: Hi Joe, good morning love, hope you slept well. This may seem very strange

JOE: You're telling me…

SARAH: but it's something we agreed to do every morning – and your doctor says that with much repetition some of what I say may register, so I want you to listen to this all the way through – and listen *properly*, Joe – none of your fast-forwarding or leaving the room with the tape still running – I know exactly what you're like, so please, please love, listen hard, this is important.

He sits on the chair listening, distractedly lighting one match after another, but never managing to light the cigarette, which is sometimes in his mouth, sometimes in his hand.

SARAH: I never know how to tell you this – and it never gets easier, even though I've done it many times, not that you'll remember… I suppose I just have to say it… You're ill, Joe – that's why you're at home listening to this and not out at work. Your brain has been injured, love, and this has affected your memory – you've got problems with your short-term memory and a form of amnesia from when you got ill two years ago. I know this will be a real shock to you but just try and listen and understand, okay? Joe? And I'll try and explain it to you technically, because I know that's how your mind works. I've left some articles on the table with your schedule, so you can read up a bit and learn what's happened to you.

JOE looks, they're there. He is distracted, not focusing.

But don't look at those now. First I'm going to explain.
Listen, Joe. Joe?

SARAH's command draws his attention back.

It all comes down to the almond and the seahorse – the amygdala and the hippocampus, components of the brain's memory circuitry, necessary for the laying down of new traces – the making of new memories. They're called the almond and the seahorse because they're shaped like that, I guess –

JOE suddenly fast forwards the tape – SARAH leaves the stage and the split stage convention ends. When JOE plays the tape again, it is a real recording.

SARAH/TAPE: ...rewired. Imagine the coloured wires in a phone line –
These wires are the axons that run from the outer layer of the brain to the cortex beneath, linking both layers of the brain and making possible the connections between the brain and the world, the brain and the body, the brain and the self.

JOE: She's lost the fucking plot.

SARAH/TAPE: With brain injury, the internal wires are separated. When – if – they reconnect it can be in haphazard or unusual ways: Red may find green, the blue wires may find yellow

Gingerly he switches it off. Sits, spooked.

JOE: Fucking hell.

He watches the tape recorder nervously, then quickly presses 'play' again.

SARAH/TAPE: – may never reconnect at all. Basically, love, you've been rewired, but in a new, illogical way.

He snaps it off, removes the tape recorder, hiding it away quickly. He sits.

JOE: Christ on a bike.

He goes to light the cigarette when an alarm on a mobile phone goes off, JOE is surprised, puts first cigarette behind his ear then goes to look for mobile phone, finds it on the table, presses snooze. He sits, starts looking through the newspaper. A pager on his belt bleeps. He takes it off, reads the message.

Take your medicine. Box in your top left pocket. Tuesday compartment.

He checks his pocket, is surprised to find the box there. He takes the pill out, goes to take it, decides he needs water. He puts the pager and the newspaper on the chair and crosses to the glass on the table. It is empty. He puts the pill separate from the box on the table. Goes to get some water, is distracted by something, puts the glass down, goes to look. Forgets what he is looking for. Stands. Sees the newspaper on the chair, goes and starts reading it. The alarm on his mobile goes again. He gets up and switches it off. Stands there. Takes out a second cigarette and puts the pack in his top left pocket. Sees the newspaper, goes to sit and read. The seat is uncomfortable, he puts the unlit cigarette in the ashtray, pulls out whatever is underneath him. It is the pager. He reads the message.

JOE: Take your medicine. Box in your top left pocket. Tuesday compartment.

He checks his pocket, no box, but finds the pack of cigarettes. He takes a third out but then sees the previous cigarette waiting in the ashtray, proof of SARAH's presence.

Sarah?

He gets up and goes to look for her, leaving both unlit cigarettes in the ashtray.

Sarah? Are you home? Is that your fag in the – ?

No SARAH. Comes back. Stands, not sure what he was doing – he was doing something… He takes out a fourth cigarette to help him think. He lights a match but sees a checklist by the phone, distracted, he blows out the light, goes there, puts the fourth unlit cigarette down in another ashtray, reads list.

'One. Take pill. Check medicine box – square, yellow –

He sees it on table, crosses to it, bringing list with him.

check Tuesday compartment. If pill there, take it. If empty, you've taken it, cross this out and go to point two.'

Fucking hilarious.

He checks the compartment, it is empty. He looks for a pen, is distracted by the pager by the chair, reads it, checks his left pocket – finds cigarettes – takes fifth out and is about to light it when he sees two out already, waiting in the ashtray. Proof of company. He goes to look.

Sarah? Sam? Are you…?

He comes back in – odd, the place is empty. He stands, takes the first cigarette from behind his ear and realises he is already holding the fifth unlit one between his fingers. He laughs at himself, puts one of the fags back in the packet, goes to light the other but before he does, the phone rings. He goes to answer it, shaking out match as he crosses, cigarette still in his hand.

Hello?… Rita?… Sorry, *Rina*, I… From India? Bloody hell, girl, it's the middle of the night over there, isn't it? What you doing calling us from there?… Oh… right…d'you like it? Does it pay well?… Okay, no problems, I – yeah, it's a bit personal, sorry… I suppose you want to speak to Sarah? Hold on a minute love and I'll get…What?... Oh, I think we get it from SWALEC, yeah…Well that's nice to know… that's really kind of…no, I'm not being funny, I mean it. There's not many people would call to say they know a cheaper electricity supplier and…yeah…okay…yeah, that sounds good… Just a minute, I'll get a pen – hold on a second.

He puts the fifth cigarette in the ashtray by the phone, starts looking for a pen, is distracted by the list on the table, picks it up and starts reading it.

…yellow box…

He checks

…empty.

He puts the box and list down – there was something else he was doing…

What was I…?

He stops, thinks, takes out a sixth fag, stands and thinks, can't remember, never mind, sees the newspaper and goes to read it. He approaches, sees the two unlit cigarettes in the ashtray – it throws him.

Sarah?

He puts cigarette number six, which he has been holding, in the ashtray, goes out and looks, comes back in, can't remember what he was doing – stands – takes out a seventh fag – sees the list on the table, goes over, reads.

You're having a fucking laugh, aren't you? Yellow box, Tuesday…

He notices the pill on the table, takes it to his lips, is about to swallow but decides he wants water. He puts the pill into the open compartment in the box, takes the glass, goes to get water, sees the phone is off the hook.

Weird…

He picks up the receiver hesitantly.

Hello?… Have I got a pen? No, I – who is this?… Rita? I don't know any Ritas… Why? Has there been a power cut?… What? Look, who is this, please?… No I haven't got a fucking pen! What's with the fucking pen? Why do you want to know if I've got a fucking…

She has hung up.

Charming. Absolutely fucking…

He goes to take out a cigarette but finds the box is empty – strange, he could have sworn it was almost half full… Suddenly a terrible noise – all the alarms go off at once. He checks his mobile, his pager, the phone starts ringing – he is rushing, hunting for the source of the noise – finds a first clock – he switches it off but a second clock alarm still rings out, escalating in decibels and volume. He finds it, can't find the off button, tries to get the batteries out, fails, tries smothering the sound, which agitates him. He starts getting desperate. His pager beeps, the alarm on his mobile sounds, the phone rings – it's sensory overload, he starts smashing up the alarm, he kicks it, smashes it against the floor rhythmically, consistently

It's not safe, it's not safe.

The phone stops ringing, as do the other alarms, but he continues to beat the clock until partway into the reverie

There's a man there's a man and he's in the water and he's drowning – drowned – and he's looking at me – I see his eye, fixed on mine – it's – but a wave carries him further out – and I'm following, I have to follow him, I nearly reach him – my hand – glistening in the water – but there's another wave and he's out further and I know it's getting dangerous – not safe, it's not safe – I'm tiring, muscles aching, I ought to go back to shore but I can't leave him – I have to reach him – he's me – he's me – I've almost got me – I've almost got me – I – I…

The phone rings, immediately breaking the tension. JOE stops, is surprised by the broken clock in his hand, rises and goes slowly to answer the phone. His mood changes immediately

Hello?… Sarah! Hiya, love…Great, no problems – yeah, and you?… What?… You're getting worse than my bloody mother. Okay, okay, I see it, a yellow box….

He takes the pill out of the right compartment

Bloody hell woman, I'm just taking it now!

He talks with the pill between his teeth.

Listen. Can you hear? This is me swallowing the pill – I've got this gorgeous sugar-coated little number in my teeth and now, listen…. Mmmmnnn, yum-yum, lovely drugs, down the little red lane, all gone. Satisfied?… Oh come on, Sarah, lighten up. Fuck's sake love, it's hardly rocket science.

9

GWENNAN in the 'garden'

GWENNAN: There's that old story my mother told me, *mae h'in wych am adrodd storiau: Y rhiain wen o'r llyn.*[10] It's a story of a man who loved The White Lady of the Lake. Now, she was beautiful and he loved her, so he pursued

10 She's a great one for the stories: The White Maiden of the Lake.

her, as any man in his right mind, in love, would. Finally she said she'd marry him, but he was never to raise his hand to her, and if he did, the third time, she'd go away – *'mi fydda i'n dy adael di.'*[11] And over the years, that's what happened – once when playing, once by accident and once in anger, he struck her – but that third time was the last time and she walked away into the lake. He woke up on the shores, an old man, his youth wasted, with all he knew and loved, perished.

10

JOE and SARAH's apartment. DR FALMER handles an archaeological artefact.

DR FALMER: Do you still go on digs?

SARAH: Not since Joe got ill.

DR FALMER: I once spent a summer excavating a site in North Wales.

SARAH: Really?

DR FALMER: Oh, years ago. I was still a student, strictly the rubble remover, poking about, longing to get my hands on a hydraulic airbrush like the real archaeologists. A summer spent digging up what turned out to be the local rubbish dump.

SARAH: You can tell a lot about a culture by what it throws away. I've often wondered what future generations will think when they dig us up. We cremate our loved ones and scatter them without leaving any marking, then commit our white goods to the earth. We'll be the spoiled generation.

DR FALMER: The selfish era.

11 I will leave you.

SARAH: Joe's at the centre today.

DR FALMER: Yes, I examined him again this morning.

SARAH: Why? Has something happened?

DR FALMER: It's just a few tests, nothing to worry about. He was on good form when I left him, using the computer in the quiet room.

SARAH: Probably bidding for some horrifically expensive non-essential on eBay. He tried to buy me a brontosaurus the other week. I keep explaining we've neither the room nor the millions and I'm not that kind of archaeologist – I'm only interested from Upright Man – but hey, what's a couple of million years between friends?

DR FALMER: You do know you can use parental controls on the internet to monitor its use?

SARAH: 'Parental'?!

DR FALMER: Partners of other patients have found it a useful option to police the sites (that are accessed by.)

SARAH: *(Interrupting.)* 'Police'? Is a theme emerging here?

DR FALMER: Only in my poor choice of words. I didn't mean to cause any offence; it was simply a suggestion to help curb any

SARAH: fun he might be having?

DR FALMER: That's not what I –

SARAH: – God knows there's little enough pleasure in Joe's life as it is without me *curbing* one of the few remaining joys of his existence.

DR FALMER: I'm sorry, I didn't –

SARAH: – Besides, I find packing things up and returning them to the stores strangely restorative. It's a sort of inverse retail therapy.

DR FALMER: Oh dear.

SARAH: No, it's fine. All part of the unpredictable, surreal experience of being with Joe. I never know if I'm dealing with a three-year-old, Nietzsche, or the Dalai Lama. He's amazing… infuriating. And I don't mean to be rude, but I'm not really sure why you're here.

DR FALMER: I want to expand our practice in the centre, to include the families and partners of patients.

SARAH: Why?

DR FALMER: Because the majority of care is given in the home and I think there's more we can do. Thirty years ago, 90% of all patients with Traumatic Brain Injury didn't survive. Now 90% do. With strokes, road accidents, tumours and since Iraq – the increase in cranial shrapnel injuries – we're fast approaching epidemic level. The majority are, like Joe, young males under the age of 35. So who's left to deal with this? You. The people at home. Understanding the situation here can help me help you and help Joe.

SARAH: So he'll improve?

DR FALMER: Further use of memory aids will certainly facilitate more independent living and –

SARAH: – He'll get better?

DR FALMER: The brain is adaptable. Studies show (there may be possible improvements…)

SARAH: *(Interrupting.)* He has to get better. At times it's like being handcuffed to a holiday rep' on acid. And people can be really cruel. They don't mean to be, it's just –

DR FALMER: – You can't see a broken brain.

SARAH: So we're given a wide berth – 'Here comes the loony – Is he on drugs? – Don't you dare touch my child'. He loves kids. Would've made a great dad, in another life, but… Oh well.

DR FALMER: How about your friends?

SARAH: I don't really see them anymore. I couldn't stomach the little smiles and pitying eyes.

DR FALMER: Perhaps you could get to know some of the other relatives at the Centre, to make a support system?

SARAH: I'm not really a joiner.

DR FALMER: It's very easy for the universe to shrink to within four walls. Really, I know. Any help from your families?

SARAH: Joe's parents have convinced themselves everything's fine, I'm over-reacting, being a hysterical woman, nothing's wrong with their golden boy… And I don't like to bother my mother. My father died last year. They were very close, so…

DR FALMER: I'm sorry.

SARAH: Thanks.

DR FALMER: It's hard, losing your father.

SARAH: Yep. And Joe doesn't know. He thinks my father's alive and that we're fine and he's the same, but… I've tried telling him, showing him stuff about the tumour – we cry, he forgets and we start all over again. And I want him to know. He'd want to know.

DR FALMER: Getting Joe to put things down in his own handwriting might help, but there could be consequences. Becoming more self-aware can bring depression, anxiety, anger –

SARAH: – Oh, great, and this for a man who can't watch the news without crying or getting angry at the pain and suffering of the world.

DR FALMER: I often wish politicians were TBI survivors – the world would be a more compassionate and just place.

SARAH: Meanwhile, pass me some of Joe's prozac.

DR FALMER: I'm sure if you went to your GP –

SARAH: – That was a joke, I wasn't serious.

DR FALMER: All the same, if you need a little extra help…

SARAH: *(Overlapping.)* I'm fine. It's just stress and tiredness. Anyway, I have my own medicine: losing myself in the safe, reliable ancient past. How ironic: the archaeologist burying herself in her work.

DR FALMER: What you're going through, it's a kind of bereavement –

SARAH: – only I still have the body, walking, talking, moving in the world almost as he was before the invasion of the body snatchers. I didn't mean that –

DR FALMER: I know.

SARAH: It's just a private joke –

DR FALMER: Of course.

SARAH: What makes you do what you do?

DR FALMER: Sorry?

SARAH: Your job. How – why – do you do this? You don't mind me asking?

DR FALMER: No. It's just I usually don't answer personal questions.

SARAH: That's funny; I thought it was a professional one.

DR FALMER: I imagine my work's not that dissimilar to yours.

SARAH: As in…?

DR FALMER: …Creating a coherent picture out of fragments. What I'm interested in is what fills that space between body and mind: Memory. It's what gives us our quality of life; it makes possible the narratives that keep our lives going forward. Without that linear structure, that link to history, life loses its richness, its connection.

SARAH: Yes.

DR FALMER: And perhaps like you, piecing together fragments, I want to create a coherent whole; I want to help find meaning.

SARAH: On my last dig, before Joe got sick, I found Elena – or, rather, she found me – tripping me up, literally. I went flying, face in the dust – and there she was: a mature female, roughly my age, not of any great interest. Females of that age and period are pretty unremarkable. But I wanted to know who she was, who had loved her so much to decorate her with shell beads and red ochre, place her on a swan's wing with her premature baby resting on her breast bone. Who had valued her, mourned her, respected her so much to bury her with such honour? I couldn't stop thinking about her. I wanted to break into the archives and steal her, put her shoulder blades back on that wing and her baby at her breast, not separated, filed and labelled in a lab'.
And I thought, who will mourn me when I'm gone? It's usually children, descendants… I always thought we'd grow old together, Joe and I, raise some kids, become one of those irritating couples like my parents, finishing each others' sentences, happily bickering and loving each other into old age. But I don't think you can do that with someone stuck in the present.
So I wait and hope.

DR FALMER: But with a realistic expectation. Look, it's easy to become isolated and depressed, divorce rates are very high and –

SARAH: – I've been deluged with images of Ganesh – the elephant faced God of disability, the remover of obstacles. And St Jude, Patron Saint of hopeless causes. And the miraculous Virgin of Guadalupe. And Beanie Babies. All these little religious icons and stuffed toys people send in a crisis – no, sorry – that females send. Men bring computer magazines and ask when Joe will be back at work and my women friends ask how he's feeling and would he like some of the Hagen Daaz they brought and left in the fridge? It's his favourite flavour…
So where do I put the Beanie Baby? On an altar, on the bed, or in the bin? Why are some icons seemingly more important or magical than others?

DR FALMER: I suppose it's the power we invest in them.

SARAH: And Bethan really believes her Beanie Baby will make Uncle Joe better. Only Uncle Joe can't remember he has a four-year-old niece. He keeps asking who the little girl is – has she wandered in from the road? Won't her mother be worried and looking for her?

DR FALMER: I know how hard it can be.

SARAH: What amazes me is how a catastrophe can so immediately undo our perception of everything. I used to be an over-qualified pain in the arse with a logical explanation for everything, noting the shifts in religious belief, the gods discarded after a technological change; identifying the rituals and sacrifices made to bargain with some higher power for rain, for a good harvest, the return to health, a miracle. I scorned it. Rationalised it. Now here I am, lighting candles, bowing to the East and believing in the healing powers of a mass-produced fabric bag filled with polystyrene balls.

11

GWENNAN in the respite centre. She senses DR FALMER observing her, as though through a two-way mirror.

GWENNAN: Sometimes I feel like an insect in an illuminated box with a magnifying lid. Or a little mammal, a shrew, or mouse, huddled against the bars of a cage.
I know they're watching me. I'm not being paranoid, there's a two-way mirror. They watch. They care. I don't mind. They can watch away, watch away all they like.
How strange. I'm under surveillance and I haven't done anything but get old.

Loud knocking is heard.
TOM paces.

I wish he'd go away.
There's nobody in. No one at home.
The room is empty.
I'm somewhere else.

12

TOM paces the corridor in the respite centre. DR FALMER approaches.

DR FALMER: I'm sorry about the other night.

TOM: What?

DR FALMER: I threatened to set the security guards on you. I'm Ife Falmer, neuropsychologist working with your wife. I'm still quite new and not yet familiar with all the relatives of the patients. Apologies. I think I probably over-reacted when you were knocking on Gwennan's door the other night.

TOM: That's fine; it's reassuring.

DR FALMER: Good. But I do think we should respect peoples' wants. Even if they have an apparent diminished capacity.

TOM: I'm not sure what you're saying…

DR FALMER: If someone doesn't want our presence, I think we should –

TOM: *(Interrupting.)* You want me to go?

DR FALMER: Of course not. Just for us to be sensitive and respectful, to compromise if necessary so we can accommodate everyone's wants and needs.

TOM: You don't want me to see my wife?

DR FALMER: I didn't say that.

TOM: You don't want me to see Gwennan?

DR FALMER: Those are not the words I would use.

TOM: But there are circumstances when you wouldn't want me to visit?

DR FALMER: Of course, if it causes distress…

TOM: And does it?

DR FALMER: Respite is there to give you both a break. It's as much for the carer's benefit as the patient's.

TOM: I cause her distress?

DR FALMER: It's a distressing situation, which I'm sure is felt on both sides. And respite is useful for partners who are also carers to take some time out, perhaps re-evaluate.

TOM: What, exactly?

DR FALMER: The future. The situation. How best to proceed from here.

It's an opportunity for you to remember yourself, focus on your own life –

TOM: – My life is on the other side of this door.

DR FALMER: No, it's not. With respect, it's here, on this side.

TOM: But –

DR FALMER: – Your wife's resting. We had a rather intense session, earlier – she'll be tired, slightly disorientated.

TOM: I cause her distress?

DR FALMER: I didn't say that.

TOM: I cause her distress?

DR FALMER: That wasn't what I meant.

He begins to walk away, returns.

TOM: What do you do when you've been obliterated, wiped out by the one person who's keeping you in this world – by the one person you're thankful every morning they're still taking breath – and they don't know you? Where does that love go?

He begins to walk away again, she watches him, he turns back.

Did knowing what my wife insisted on calling 'the language of Heaven' keep the words in her head? Did being bilingual save her from having aphasia?

DR FALMER: Potentially, I don't know. We'll never know. Playing the cello may have helped. A neuroscientist can immediately recognise a musician simply by looking at their brain scan. It has a tangible physical impact, not associated with any other art or skill. And musical memory is often retained when all other forms of memory are lost.

TOM: She seems to get comfort just from having the cello in the room. And when she still played – years ago, now – she seemed the same, untouched by her injury.

DR FALMER: It reanimates. Playing music can enrich and expand existence. And when that existence is from moment to moment, outside time in an unstructured limbo, it can create stability. Even joy.

TOM: But we can't force her to play.

DR FALMER: No. And the outcome is impossible to predict. No brain is the same. No brain sustains injury in the same way.

TOM: And every brain bleeds differently.

DR FALMER: Yes. Because of a small bleed, the tiniest lesion, someone's life-long passion – gardening, say, is gone. Wiped out, no longer accessible on the hard drive of the organic computer-mind. No more baby's breath, love in a mist, tulips, or heart's ease. Goodbye, daisies. Still, there are worse things.

TOM: I'm sorry, I don't…

DR FALMER: Brain injury is a reconfiguration. The more RAM of memory a person had, the more powerful the processor – say a Pentium – the better chance that the system will work reasonably well after it crashes, once the hard drive has been defragmented.

TOM: I know you're trying to be helpful and I'm male which might make you suppose certain knowledge and information is available to me, but I'm a bit of a luddite who hates humans being compared to machines.

DR FALMER: Fine. I better skip the car analogy and faulty rear brake light, then.

TOM: Please do.

DR FALMER: Let's start again?
What metaphor are you working with?

TOM: Sorry?

DR FALMER: What analogy or image – what vehicle are you using to represent your wife's condition?

TOM: I'm not.

DR FALMER: Really?

TOM: Is there something wrong with that?

DR FALMER: No, it's just that's generally how we understand that which is incomprehensible. We use images and tell ourselves stories to bring order to the chaos, to understand the unfathomable.

TOM: I don't believe in God, either.

DR FALMER: Fine.

TOM: Or life after death or the existence of the soul. We're just electrical impulses, carbon matter.

DR FALMER: Motorised meat.

TOM: Yes, though I can see why the families of your other patients might prefer the organic computer analogy.

DR FALMER: Quite.

TOM: I used to think we were unique – individual souls or selves or minds… I used to think that was where the self lay – behind the eyes – where the consciousness, personality, 'essence' lived, rattling around inside an obedient shell. There's no ghost in the machine. If we can get hit on the head and become a different person, what does that tell us about being human? And the poor brain, it thinks it's a soul; it thinks it's immortal.

He begins to walk away again, stops, speaks from a distance.

What do I do?

13

SARAH and JOE at home at the end of the day:

SARAH: So how was your day?

JOE: I don't know.

SARAH: The sense of it, then – the flavour, the aftertaste.

JOE: Alright, I think.

SARAH: What did you do?

JOE: You're asking me what I did today?

SARAH: Just one thing.

JOE: I don't know.

SARAH: Check your diary, then. I'm sure you'll have written something down.

JOE: Fuck off.

SARAH: One thing.

JOE: Fuck off.

SARAH: Just one –

JOE: – I robbed a bank. Then I released all the penguins out of Bristol zoo, had lunch with the first minister and found a cure for cancer on my return journey from the Assembly.

SARAH: That's great!

JOE: I wasn't being serious, Sarah.

SARAH: But it's irony, a higher brain function, needing two levels of thought and the wit to discriminate between them.

JOE: Do you think I'm stupid?

SARAH: No.

JOE: So why are you using that voice?

SARAH: Sorry?

JOE: I hate it when you speak to me in that voice.

SARAH: That –?

JOE: – Patronising, schoolteacher voice.

SARAH: It's not intentional. I'm sorry. I… Where's your schedule? You know you're supposed to have it with you at all times.

JOE: – There it is! That voice – that –

SARAH: – I'm doing the best I can, here.

JOE: I hate that voice.

SARAH: Well tough – because it's the only one I've got.

She finds the schedule.

And here…your schedule – which should be with you at all times! How many times do I have to tell you?

JOE: Fuck's sake, okay!

SARAH: I'm sorry – I….

JOE: Christ.

SARAH: Joe, please – it's really important. You can navigate by this – it allows you to have some kind of life. At any time when you're not sure where you are or what you're supposed to be doing, you simply look at the time and then in the schedule and it will tell you. So you won't get scared –

JOE: Behave.

SARAH: – there'll be no panic attacks and I won't get stressed out worrying about you. Okay? Are you listening? Joe?

JOE: Do you think we can dream our children before they're conceived?

SARAH: What?

JOE: Do they exist out there, in the mass of energy and molecular particles that is the universe, out there beyond, in the dark that isn't really dark, just waiting to choose their parents, the family to be born into?

SARAH: Just when I think you're gone, there's a flash and you're back and –

JOE: – Soul families… But not in the James Brown sense.

SARAH: – and then you're gone again.
I suppose it's comforting, the notion of reincarnation – that there's a finite number of souls and we just keep recycling, coming round again but in different combinations of our messy fuck-ups… And maybe a part of us does continue after death? Every culture has a philosophy of afterlife, of becoming one with the universe. And something can't just become nothing, can it?

JOE: I'll have to consult my old physics teacher on that.

SARAH: If human matter is compacted energy, where else could that energy or 'soul' go after death, except back to the place it was before birth?

JOE: Bloody hell, it's Mystic Meg!

SARAH: Well it can't all just go to waste – can it? All that knowledge and experience and pain. It has to be for something. It's too cruel if we've gone through all this for nothing.

JOE: Through what?

SARAH: I wonder what my lesson is this time round? No, it's penance. I'm doing penance. I must've been a mass murderer in a previous life.

JOE: Or a puppy killer.

SARAH: Exactly.

JOE: A drowner of kittens. One of those vicious children who pull wings off flies and lock their teachers in broom cupboards over the Bank Holiday weekend.

SARAH: I've got the idea.

JOE: The kind of hooligan that leaves razor blades in bars of soaps in public loos and releases spores of nasty diseases over the salad bars in Pizza huts.

SARAH: I really want a baby, Joe. No, not *a, our* baby.
I want your child, Joe. But is it possible?
Could I manage?
And the child – how would she negotiate being…
Are you listening? Did you hear what I said?
Are you actually still in there? Joe?

JOE: What?

SARAH: It's like something's been extinguished– in your eyes – they're different.

JOE: Have you been at the cooking sherry?

SARAH: I miss your eyes – your old eyes – the eyes that were connected to your original brain.

JOE: I don't know what gets into you, sometimes.

SARAH: I miss you.

JOE: Now you're just being stupid.

SARAH: I really miss you, Joe.

JOE: Hello? I'm here.

SARAH: No, you're not.

JOE: What's this then? What's this?

SARAH: You're not the same.

JOE: I am here. I'm fucking here!

SARAH: No. You're kind and well-meaning and weirdly likeable, but… You're not bitter and twisted and cynical, dark in the soul the way you used to be. And I loved that. It wasn't always comfortable, but I knew I was alive.

JOE: Are you having some kind of breakdown, an existential crisis?

SARAH: Probably.

JOE: That's what comes from spending your life digging up corpses – my mother always said it was morbid. She never understood what I saw in you – what's a plumber got in common with an archaeologist?

SARAH: Well, I'm basically an archivist now and you haven't worked in two years. You kept leaving jobs undone – flooding peoples' houses, installing showers incorrectly…

JOE: What is wrong with you today?

SARAH: *Today*… now that really is an interesting one… The construct of Time combined with human consciousness…

JOE: What…?!

SARAH: Some mathematicians would say there is no such thing as the passing of time – the future, just as the past, is a subjective concept and all we really have is the moment – this moment – the one we breathe in now…now… I understand the theory – the relics and the human remains I work with are alive to me –

JOE: - Sarah…

SARAH: – they're not dead, or of the past – they're current, present, and perhaps if I could really be in the moment, it'd work between you and me –

JOE: – Stop it

SARAH: But it can't work.

JOE: I mean it, Sarah – stop this –

SARAH: There's a tension between the two periods of time I personally inhabit: Joe Time and Real Time –

JOE: – fuck's sake…

SARAH: – and I travel back and forth between them, trying to keep sane.

JOE: What's going on? What the fuck is wrong with you?

SARAH: Read your book.

JOE: Something's happened…

SARAH: Read it in your book.

JOE: I'm sure something's happened.

SARAH: You're right. Something did. You wrote it down in your book. Read your list, Joe.

JOE: But what happened?

SARAH: It's in your book. The Important information for Joe by Joe.

JOE: What?

SARAH: Read your list, Joe. There, in your book.

JOE: But –

SARAH: Read your fucking list, Joe. It's in your book, read your fucking book, Joe.

JOE: *(reads)* 'Important Information About Your Broken Brain –What the –?!

SARAH: Read it.

JOE: *(reads)* 'Important Information About Your Broken Brain For Joe By Joe: One, I am you and we have been ill. Two, we grew a tumour the size of an orange inside our skull, but it's okay, it was benign. Three, they removed the tumour and with it large sections of our memory…'

What the fuck is this?

SARAH: Do you recognise the handwriting?

JOE: Yeah.

SARAH: Whose is it?

JOE: It's – it looks like mine.

SARAH: Well then.

JOE: Well then what?

SARAH: Don't you remember?

JOE: What's to remember?

SARAH: What happened.

JOE: None of this is making any sense and I…

SARAH: It's your handwriting.

JOE: I can't do this. I can't do this. And it's my fault, yes, I'm sorry, I'm really sorry, I fucked up – I know I did something wrong, I messed everything up, I did, I'm to blame, I'm to blame, I'm –

SARAH calms JOE

SARAH: No, it's not your fault, you didn't do anything. It was just fate or meant or bad luck or predestined or –

(They comfort each other.)

I've been having these thoughts that are really frightening: What if God does exist but is indifferent, or simply hates us?

14

TOM outside GWENNAN's 'door' in the respite centre

TOM: Gwen? Gwennie?
It's me. It's – don't open the door, just… listen, all right love?
I'm sorry. I'm so sorry, I didn't mean to upset you earlier, I never do mean to, but – I know you find yourself in a frightening,

confusing place and you get scared so you lock yourself away and then suddenly you hear a familiar voice at the door so you rush to open it but when you do, the face doesn't match the voice, the face is strange, it belongs to someone else and that makes you even more frightened. And I'm sorry. I'm sorry that I've changed. I'm sorry that you don't know me anymore.
They say the body renews itself every seven years – every cell is replaced. If that's true, this is just a memory speaking to another memory.
I'm sorry, my love. I don't think we should do this anymore.
I'm so sorry, I'm –

He leaves and walks along some of the pathways.

15

GWENNAN in the respite centre.

GWENNAN: There was once a woman walking along a shore. It was twilight, her eyes patchy in the light. She could see another lone figure like her walking towards her and as they grew nearer, she could see it was a young woman. And as they grew closer, she could see how she walked and it was familiar, a way of moving so reminiscent of someone she knew. And as they were about to pass, the woman saw that it was her younger self. 'Go back', she cried, '*dos nol. Dos nol.*'[12]

16

TOM and SARAH meet on one of the pathways in the grounds outside the centre. She is putting a cigarette out.

TOM: That'll kill you, you know.

12 Go back. Go back.

SARAH: – Which is why I like to smoke alone and in silence, honouring the fat deposits clogging my veins, the carcinogens collecting in the bottom of my lungs. Some things have to be done with full awareness and concentration. It's a talent, some would say discipline: total commitment when in the slow process of self-annihilation.

TOM: I've never been one for small talk, either.

SARAH: I only do monologue.

They look towards the centre

TOM: It changes you.

They exchange a glance and part, SARAH heading for DR FALMER's office.

17

DR FALMER's office. SARAH enters. DR FALMER is waiting for her:

SARAH: They said you –

DR FALMER: Come in.

SARAH: I disturbed –?

DR FALMER: Not at all.

SARAH: I can come (back later.) –

DR FALMER: Please, sit down.

SARAH remains standing

SARAH: I came to get Joe but was told you wanted to speak with me?

DR FALMER: That's right. I'd like to keep Joe in the residential wing for a while –

SARAH: – But he always comes home with me and

DR FALMER: Shouldn't be for too long. I'd just like to do a few more tests, keep him under observation.

SARAH: Is there a problem?

DR FALMER: Please, sit down.

SARAH remains standing

SARAH: Is there a problem?

DR FALMER: According to Joe's medical notes, he has no memory or recollection of anything in the last two years.

SARAH: That's right.

DR FALMER: I currently estimate his most recent memory as being from thirty to thirty-six months ago.

SARAH: I don't really understand –

DR FALMER: I'm concerned about a possible erosion of Joe's existing memories going back to before the tumour.

SARAH: I'm sorry, I –

DR FALMER: Joe's autobiographical memory appears to be deteriorating.

SARAH: His memory's deteriorating. *(She sits.)*

DR FALMER: It seems so.

SARAH: He's slipping further back into the past?

DR FALMER: I can't say for sure at the moment, but I think so, yes.

SARAH: He's rewinding?

DR FALMER: Yes.

SARAH: Deleting his memories?

DR FALMER: I'm sorry.

SARAH: So when will it stop? When is it going to stop?

DR FALMER: It's impossible to say.

SARAH: So is he just going to carry on rewinding, erasing – our lives?

DR FALMER: I really can't say at the moment –

SARAH: What if he rewinds back to before we met? Is it possible?

DR FALMER: I –

SARAH: He won't know me; he'll have deleted everything, wiped us out, every experience, every… No.

DR FALMER: I'm sorry.

SARAH: I thought there was still hope. You told me there was still hope.

DR FALMER: No, I didn't actually, I –

SARAH: – All those memory aids, exercises, recordings. Joe's schedule–

DR FALMER: – All designed to facilitate and support independent living.

SARAH: 'The brain is adaptable' you said.

DR FALMER: Yes, it is, but –

SARAH: You gave me hope.

DR FALMER: But always tempered with a reasonable expectation…

SARAH: He's not going to improve. Joe's never going to get better.

DR FALMER: I'm sorry. I do understand what you're going through, I –

SARAH: How can you?

DR FALMER: I thought it could help – I wanted to try –

SARAH: – Experiments, little mice in a cage, that's all we are to you. You don't know how it feels –

DR FALMER: – I do, I –

SARAH: You gave me hope and you shouldn't have. You shouldn't have given me hope.

DR FALMER: But –

SARAH leaves the office

I didn't.

SARAH rushes from the office. She encounters TOM on a pathway. There is a moment of connection – a glance, a look, an understanding. Slowly they begin to move towards one another.

The lights dim on them, and rise on DR FALMER in her office:

DR FALMER sits, facing her computer. She scrolls down her previous pages – jargon and medical terms – then writes

DR/TYPE: My father was a brilliant man, a horticulturist and botanist, but at the end of his life –

She pauses, then types/speaks.

DR/TYPE: No one thinks of the family, of the bewildered relatives left to

She stops and then deletes, letter by letter, using backspace, all she has written.

18

SARAH with TOM. The morning after the night before.

SARAH: Could you pass me a towel? For a shower? I'd like to freshen up before I leave and –

TOM: – Towel?

SARAH: *(Fast.)* An oblong piece of absorbent material with which to blot water from my naked skin following ablutions.

TOM: That's impressive. Do you breathe through the skin?
Don't you need to pause and inhale like us lesser mortals?

SARAH: No. Scary, isn't it? Despite the fags, excellent breath control. I can go on for hours, if I need to. All those words, meaningless, hot air, pumped out – pa-pa-pa-pa-pa-pa-pa-pa – ammunition. Sometimes I feel like a tommy gun.

TOM: Tommy gun?

SARAH: Kalashnikov – rapid repeat rifle – an automatic weapon spraying the air with bullets of useless words. It's not very effective, they're just sounds, that's all.

TOM: About last night…

SARAH: Don't.
Look: I'm not in the habit of doing this, so just forget, just forget the whole – I'll have a shower and be out of your life and

TOM: I don't believe there's any crime in giving comfort.

SARAH: That's a new one. I haven't heard it called that before.

TOM: But that's what we did, see. We comforted each other.
We both needed one another last night and if you want to beat yourself up about it, that's fine. And if you want to blame me for what happened, that's also fine; I'll accept responsibility. But don't ask me to regret it. And Sarah, don't dirty it. I was desperate last night and you were so kind, you cared for me, you showed me more warmth than any other human being has in years.

SARAH: So you need to get out more.

TOM: You understood I was in need of consoling.

SARAH: And that's what I was – consolation?

TOM: No, more, much more than that. Sarah, I feel alive, I feel… Oh, come here.

SARAH: I'm not sure, I –

TOM: Let me hold you.

SARAH: I –

TOM: Please.

(Pause.)

I used to watch you at the centre, walking in, smiling, imprint of your teeth on your lower lip like you'd been biting down, hard. I'd see you drop him off for a few hours break – almost bolting for the door once you handed him over, full of guilt and recriminations – I know, I understand, we've more in common than you think. And until the other day, I've never heard you say more than a sentence. Not that I'm complaining. I like hearing you talk. I'm used to silence, or tears, a locked door and hearing myself talk through it, hating myself, mumbling on in some pathetic monologue, rehashing the past, serving it up cold with a stupid garnish like 'the weather today, it really reminds me of when we met thirty years ago' – because what else is there to talk of? What else have I done? I gave up work to look after Gwennan, our friends left, family passed on and I was left here, romanticising 'the way we were' – the way she was, before. And I don't even know if it's true anymore. Did we really love like that? Was that the person she was, or have I just invented her?

But now there's someone who understands, who knows what it's like, who –

(SARAH breaks away.)

What?

SARAH: I'm sorry, this isn't what I want.

TOM: But –

SARAH: I'm not prepared to turn this into some kind of carers' self-help group. Oh, I know I'll miss all those hours of fun comparing notes, sharing those special zombie moments –

TOM: – Why are you being like this?

SARAH: Because I was trying to get away from it all last night, because last night was supposed to be about me, because I'm sleeping with strange men, and I include my husband Joe in that and because he looks at me sometimes with this Midwich Cuckoo face and… You don't know what it's like.

TOM: Try me.

SARAH: He looks at me sometimes and it's like the lights are on but someone else is home. What makes him him is…it's…

TOM: …missing.

SARAH: Yes.

TOM: The last time I saw Gwennie was in our car over twenty years ago. She was smiling at me, four months pregnant, buckling the seat belt over our bump – tiny, it was, barely visible – and that was the second before the car swung out and cannoned into us, sending her through the windscreen.
That's our life, forever crashing through the windscreen.
I never saw her again.
Wherever she went, she never came back.
They sent someone else.

(Pause.)

What happens when you come to the end of the line and there are no babies to tell the stories to? Or there are no stories, as the archive has perished, the memory banks burst and everything lost. What happens then? Does it matter?

SARAH: I don't know.

TOM: I want it to matter. Nothing will last, of me. I sometimes think that's all we are, that's all there is: genetic code and a string of anecdotes. Well, I'm buggered on both counts. We lost our one chance.

SARAH: But you could still –

TOM: – Not with Gwennan. She doesn't even know who I am anymore.

SARAH: There may be other options, other possibilities….

TOM: Might there be, Sarah?

SARAH: What?

TOM: Other options, other possibilities?
Sarah?

SARAH: I don't know.

19

The respite centre. JOE is copying the articles from scene 8 into his book and looking over previous pages.

JOE: 'The present is given meaning by its relationship and connection to the past: The remembered present.'
I look at the words…my handwriting… My hand held the pen which left these markings.
I wrote these sentences:
The doctor said I am to write things down.
Sarah is crying again.
I'm making her miserable.
I don't remember, I don't fucking remember.
I wrote the date on the top right hand corner of each page. I wrote these – but I don't remember.
'The present is given meaning by its relationship and connection to the past: the remembered present. Each moment is

given potential and tension by the future. Like mountain ranges or marks on a graph – without that past and future, there is just a flat line – that is, life is flat but complete, in each moment.'
Life is flat but complete, in each moment.
If I write it, I remember. I put it together again. I re-member.
Without past and future, there is a flat line.
I'm a flatliner. Does that mean I'm dead? Am I dead? Am I?
In the water, drowning, there's a man. In the water, a man and he looks like me – he's a flatliner – he's a… It's no longer safe – I'm no longer safe, it's no longer safe, no longer safe –

DR FALMER observes. SARAH rushes in, tries to comfort him.

SARAH: It's alright, Joe, it's alright –

JOE: I want to speak to Sarah.

SARAH: I'm here.

JOE: I want to call her.

SARAH: Joe, I'm here.

JOE: I want the other Sarah.
The real one.
The one that's at home.

DR FALMER stands, watching.

SARAH gives JOE her mobile, he dials and gets the answer-machine.

JOE: Sarah, this is your husband speaking.
I'm really sorry I missed you – you're probably out shopping, or at work – I can't remember your schedule this week. Anyway, I'm thinking of you – I miss you – and just thought I'd call and tell you that. I really hope to see you soon. Call me when you get in. I love you.

He hands the mobile to SARAH, who hangs up. JOE returns to his task, SARAH ignored and apparently unrecognised. SARAH slowly exits.

20

DR FALMER's office. She is working on her notes for her lecture

DR FALMER: ...after all the work we've made on ourselves to grow, develop, be successful, a better person – at the end, or following an accident or illness, we can be held captive to our earliest memories. We think we're in control, then we're ambushed by time. A lifetime of learning, achieving wisdom and knowledge – wiped out, obliterated. Our experiences are deleted, our relationships erased

She breaks away from her notes.

and what a waste, what a bloody...

My father was a brilliant man, a botanist and horticulturist, yet at the end of his life he was unable to identify a common daisy growing on the lawn...

No one thinks of the family, of the bewildered relatives left to make sense of this wreck, this ruin of what was, the splendour, gone, the...

She speaks, typing:

We should not invest so in such perishable goods.

The words are visible, projected.

We should not invest so in such perishable goods.
We should not invest so in such perishable goods.
We should not invest so in such perishable goods.
We should not invest so in such perishable goods.

She stands and begins to pack her briefcase, preparing to leave.

GWENNAN stands in the doorway, watching.

GWENNAN: I know something now, which I won't, at other times.

They look at one another.

I know I'm older than I thought I was. Time's passing, life's moving on; I'm getting older. But tomorrow morning, I'll be a young girl.

DR FALMER: And then you'll have to go through all this, all over again.

GWENNAN: Yes.
Yes I will.
Yes.

DR FALMER looks at GWENNAN. Then she puts down her briefcase and sits.

21

TOM and SARAH. Early morning.

TOM: So you're awake, then.

SARAH: Sleepwalking.

TOM: You seem pretty awake to me.

SARAH: I'm good at deceiving. Particularly myself. Bruce Chatwin wrote somewhere that archaeologists committed suicide more than any other profession because by dealing with the past, we could see and couldn't resist, our inevitable extinction.

TOM: It's not even six thirty.

SARAH: So?

TOM: Bit early, isn't it?

SARAH: For…?

TOM: That kind of talk.

SARAH: But not sex, perhaps.

TOM: That's not what I –

SARAH: – Isn't it?

TOM: No! I didn't –

SARAH: – No?

TOM: No!

(Pause.)

SARAH: So if I was to ask you – only hypothetically, of course – what would you be your preferred route of doing away with yourself, what would you say?

TOM: For Christ's sake.

SARAH: Well?

TOM: I wouldn't.

SARAH: Russian roulette, I think – then you can entertain yourself as you go. No – injecting air into a vein like the nurses in the Boer war did when the morphine had run out – a perfect bubble of death sailing along in your bloodstream, particularly good for those who like anticipation.

TOM: Life has a way of erasing us anyway. It doesn't need my help.

SARAH: I think my mother's slowly poisoning herself. Just half an aspirin too much every day… apparently it can take up to a year to take effect, but she's organised. She misses my father and wants to go to him.

Beat.

What do you do when you're grieving but no one has physically died?

TOM: Sarah….

SARAH: You're not him.

TOM: I know.

SARAH: You're not him.

TOM: I know.

SARAH: You're not him.

Beat.

We're not very good at this, are we?

TOM: No.

SARAH: I've tried

TOM: Yes

SARAH: but I just keep seeing his face.

TOM: I know.

SARAH: It's torture.

TOM: Sometimes I feel like we're separated by a glass wall. I'm on one side and Gwennan's on the other –

SARAH: – only it's not glass – it's ice.

TOM: Yes. She's caught in a huge block of ice and there's no thawing– she's encased, and alive and there's nothing I can do.

SARAH: There's absolutely nothing I can do but watch him.

TOM: Yes. Just stand back and…

SARAH: … A flashback relationship – this little bubble of anecdotes within which we have our emotional life. We're not trying to revisit our past

TOM: – we're stuck in it –

SARAH: and if I want to have any kind of emotional intimacy with Joe, that's where I have to go. Backwards. When my real life is moving forwards and –

TOM: But it isn't. Is it Sarah? We're not moving forwards.

SARAH: No, we're not.
And that's what we're all supposed to do nowadays, isn't it? Move on? Isn't that the phrase, the current psychobabble? 'Seek closure.' Seize your life and live it, 'cause we're only here once and I know how long you can be a corpse; I've dug enough of them up over the years – and there was nothing there except bone and ash…
I thought different, once. It was alive – the artefacts, belief systems, culture – significant. It was like a rope of DNA, a link through time. Things had meaning. They were connected. I could piece it all together and see eternity. But now it's just a loop –

TOM: Her face and a locked door.

SARAH: I don't see eternity anymore. Just a wipe clean board.

TOM: I want a future.

SARAH: Be content with the present. We're here, now.

TOM: No we're not.

Pause.

SARAH: Tom, hold me. Please? Tom?

He moves away from her.

What happened to the man who comforted me, who understood?

TOM: He grew old and disappeared.

22

The grounds of the respite centre. JOE is disorientated and alone.

JOE: Outside. Garden. Tree. Familiar…
Neighbour's tree? No. Parents' tree? Wrong kind. Not our tree, we don't have a garden. I… Outside. Garden. Fuck… Check hands.

Hands cold. Check pockets. List? Money? Instructions? Hands: empty. Going in or coming out? Hands: cold. Coming back, going in. But *empty* hands – no bags, no shopping, no… Sarah? No. Check pockets. Schedule? Watch: two thirty-six. Instructions? Going in or coming out? Outside, in a garden, by a tree. Schedule…? Instructions? Shopping? No – visiting – yes, visiting. Shit. Who the hell am I visiting? Keys… Did I lock the door? Did I lock –? Am I going in? Returning? Yes, returning: hands cold, long walk. Returning – where? In a garden, by a fucking tree. Check hands, pockets – fuck!

GWENNAN approaches

GWENNAN: Are you all right?

JOE: Oh! I –

GWENNAN: – Didn't mean to startle –

JOE: – No! You… Hello!

GWENNAN: Hello.

JOE: I'm Joe.

GWENNAN: Gwennan.

JOE: Lovely garden you have here, Gwennan. Mature.

GWENNAN: It's not mine.

JOE: No? D'you know whose it is?

GWENNAN: Not really, no.

JOE: Well, we're in the same boat, then. I hate this – social occasions – someone's party and I don't know who the host is.

GWENNAN: Maybe you're lost? We're in the grounds of a health centre.

JOE: Was I in an accident?

GWENNAN: I don't think so; you look fine.

JOE: So why am I here?

GWENNAN: Visiting someone?

JOE: That'll be it. I'm probably here with my other half – Sarah? Ring any bells? No? Good! Shit.

GWENNAN: Sorry, should I know you?

JOE: Probably. Who's to know? You can never tell, you –
I like the garden.

GWENNAN: Yes.

JOE: Mature trees. Vegetation. Plants. Grass. That's nice in a garden. Shit, I'm stuffed. I – excuse the language.

GWENNAN: It's fine. Not that I like swearing. I didn't mean to startle you. Earlier, I mean.

JOE: No, no… It's nice to see you.

GWENNAN: And you.

JOE: Hello.

GWENNAN: You're very familiar.

JOE: That's because I am, see. A little too over-familiar at times, I think. If that's the case, just tap me on the wrist and…

She is looking at him intently.

What? Do I have something on my face?

GWENNAN: – No – you just remind me of someone.

JOE: I've got one of those faces – common –

GWENNAN: – archetypal.

JOE: I always have people saying I remind them of someone; usually their nephew, younger brother or –

GWENNAN: – My husband.

JOE: Oh!

GWENNAN: It's not so much a facial resemblance, but something… I don't know, maybe it's to do with your height or age or…

JOE: Ooh… Got yourself a toy boy did you?

GWENNAN: No! He's about our age.

JOE: Our…?

GWENNAN is easily fifteen years older than JOE. He is at a loss as to what to say – so says nothing. Several beats.

GWENNAN: D'you think he's gone?

JOE: Sorry –?

GWENNAN: The man. Will you look? That's why I came out here, to hide in the garden.

JOE: Is it a game?

GWENNAN: No. I think he was about to leave, so I slipped out here.
He might have followed me and I really don't want to turn around, so… Can you see anyone behind me?

JOE: No.

GWENNAN: There's nobody at all standing behind me?

JOE: No.

GWENNAN: So he's gone?

JOE: Who?

GWENNAN: The man.

JOE: Has someone hurt you?

GWENNAN: No, no… He's kind, actually very kind, but I don't really know him. He's familiar to look at – but….older. He claims he's – but no, he's too old for that.

JOE: So… Hello…

GWENNAN: I disturbed you.

JOE: No.

GWENNAN: You were talking to yourself – or maybe meditating, praying… I didn't want to interrupt – it's rude – I just didn't want to see the man. They tell me that when he goes he likes to say goodbye to me but it makes him upset and I don't like that.

JOE: I'm Joe.

GWENNAN: I know.

JOE: Hello.

GWENNAN: Hello, Joe, I'm Gwennan.

JOE: Hello.

(Pause.)

What do we do, now?

GWENNAN: We could sit down, have a chat – maybe over a cup of tea?

JOE: I'd like that.

GWENNAN: I hope you don't think I'm being forward…..

JOE: Just as long as you don't tell my girlfriend.

GWENNAN: Or my husband.

JOE: Well I won't if you won't.

GWENNAN: And neither of them seems to be here, so we're safe.

JOE: I feel safe.

(Beat.)

What do we do now?

GWENNAN: We go in and maybe I'll play something for you…?

JOE: Are you a musician?

GWENNAN: Yes. The cello.

A distant, resounding chord from the cello.

JOE: The cello?

GWENNAN: Yes.

JOE: You know something? I'd like that.

Slow fade to the sound of Bach's Sarabande.

End of play.

In Water I'm Weightless

Performance script for Unlimited Commission/National Theatre Wales production, part of the 2012 Cultural Olympiad.

Originally developed as 'The 'd' Monologues.

'…thrillingly vitriolic…'

The Guardian

'…a powerful piece of theatre, shattering any stereotypes...a thought-provoking, beautiful piece of theatre which makes you realise that everyone is unique – and equal…'

The Western Mail

'…What sets *In Water I'm Weightless* apart is that although disability is the topic of choice, the play transcends this…depict[ing] lives filled with emotion, circumstance and a vulnerability that everyman can identify with. This is a celebration of humanity, of the body, of character and resilience, in all forms… provocative and stimulating…'

The Public Reviews

An Unlimited commission for the Cultural Olympiad and London 2012 Festival, produced by National Theatre Wales at Wales Millennium Centre and Southbank Centre, *In Water I'm Weightless* premiered at WMC on 26 July 2012.

Cast

Mandy Colleran

Mat Fraser

Karina Jones

Nick Phillips

Sophie Stone

David Toole

Sign language interpreters	Jo Ross Julie Hornsby
Visual language expert	Jean St Clair
Director	John Mcgrath
Producer	Lucy Davis
Designer	Paul Clay
Movement Director	Nigel Charnock
Associate Choreographer	Catherine Bennett
Emerging director	Sara Beer

I'm Sorry

I'm sorry.

I'm so, so sorry. It will happen to you.

It will happen on a specific date at a
fragmented hour and immediately
everything you know will change.

It will happen slowly, so inconsequentially
that you will not notice until a moment
before it is upon you and there is nothing
you will be able to do to avoid it.

It will happen in slow motion, in the second
the metal of the car slams into the flesh of
your body. The cells and the sinews and
the crushed blood vessels and the synapses
clicking and you going 'oh, oh,' knowing
it has happened as you spiral and hit the
tarmac, but still not really believing it – that
horror, that churning horror as you realise
it's not going to be a happy ending, after all.

There are no happy endings.

There are only endings.

But before the endings, sometimes a great
length of time before the actual endings,
there is the moment of change.

Sometimes it is swift and shrill and cunning –
in on and away and nothing will be the same
again.

Sometimes it is slow – so slow and slight the
accumulation, you are not aware until it has
passed the point of return – if ever there is a
point from which return is possible.

Once change happens, there's no going back.
No. You have been changed by what your
tissues have known, what the molecules have

experienced. There is no return to innocence or inexperience.

I'm sorry, but it will happen to you in a moment's carelessness – the groping foot on the stair after one drink too many; the nudge from a passing stranger that knocks you off kilter and into the traffic, the thoughtless tuning of the radio which facilitates the impact at thirty miles an hour and them saying you came from nowhere and they didn't even see you.

It will happen by a dulling, slow and daily, over so many hours that perhaps friends and family will notice the ultimate betrayal first – your own body turning against you.

It will happen suddenly one morning with the smell of burning rubber and the numbness of your feet on the cold bedroom floor.

It will happen in a heartbeat.

It will happen with the steady growth of moss on trees in a forest.

It will happen with the shrill immediacy of a siren starting up, landlocked in traffic.

It will happen.

I'm sorry. I don't know when it will happen, but it will happen to you.

It will.

I'm sorry.

It will happen.

Fragments on a fragmentary vision

Columbus got it wrong. The world is flat.
Without dimension, but such colour, shapes.

How do we describe seeing?

Definition: See. Verb. Have or use power of perceiving with eye; descry; observe; look at; discern mentally; be passive spectator of.

My sight is not passive. It is maverick, flattening the world with a stroke of the retina. Buildings fall into straight lines at my glance; at my mercurial eye the earth trembles. Like Lear, I strike flat the thick rotundity of the world.

I walk down the road, not knowing if the car before me is moving or stationary.

I walk down the road with my bird-like cranings – the tilt of the jerking head, the eye monitoring, deceiving, explaining, deciphering.

Was that a black cat or just a blind spot crossing my path? Forever optimistic. A cat, it was. I will be in luck today.

No, it was a manhole, uncovered. I fall down. I will still be in luck today.

How do we describe seeing?

Definition: Fragmentary. Broken (Latin fragmantum; French, frangere, to break.)

My sight is not broken. It is clear. Pure. Shards of vision, of light, converged in my mind's eye.

My sight is not broken. Rather, it breaks the world.

Transition:

I love pulling into the disabled parking space, music pumping, sunnies on, seeing all those disapproving faces, deciding when I'll reveal the blue badge and wheels…

'Oh, sorry mate, I didn't realise you were a DISABLED. It's just I didn't know you had a wheelchair. You didn't look DISABLED.'

Random Growth

Split scene convention. This spoken text is performed by three actors, with similar text simultaneously signed by two other performers.

1: When I was younger – teens, perhaps – people always asked me what I wanted to be when I grew up.

2: It's like that flat pack furniture from Ikea.

1: What I wanted to be? 'Whole' I would say. 'A real, full boy' –

3: I don't think I ever felt broken.

1: – because being fragmented didn't feel *real.*

2: You know how it is when you cart it all home and spend forever putting it together with a variety of fiddly bolts in those splintery holes, tightened with strange, tiny spanners –

1: Or not *real* like the stories in soaps seemed *real.*

2: – and then it just slumps, or won't stand up on its own –

3: *Broken* suggested you had all the pieces to begin with.

2: – has some kind of technical fault you need an expert to advise you on, or have to send it back, faulty, to the manufacturers…?

1: 'Fragmented' as that's how I felt, even before I really knew the word or what it meant.

2: Well I suppose it was like that when my bewildered parents got me home in the Moses basket, still smelling of newness and hope and Mothercare. Only they couldn't return me to the faulty goods department. They had me. For good.

1: Disappointment is the word that springs to mind.

2: Not that my parents ever said such to me –

1: – which, as a teenager, made me feel even more apart.

3: All my friends were having great, operatic rows with their parents about how disappointing they were as offspring, and they'd never have gone to all that trouble and expense of having them if they'd known for just one second how they'd turn out.

1: Which was not a phrase my parents could ever say to me, of course.

2: Even though I wished they would.

1: Even though they thought it – I could tell.

3: You can smell disappointment.

2: It rises up like unwashed sheets in an unmade bed.

1: So maybe that's what I was – unmade –

2: Or maybe like my mother said when I was a child and asked why I am as I am:

3: 'You just needed to stay a little longer in the oven, sweetheart. You're not quite 'done' in the middle.'

1: I've often wondered what kind of food I might have been:

3: A soufflé

1: Or baked alaska.

2: Surely not a bun, or a loaf, that would be too clichéd –

1: – all kneady and blanched and soggy in the middle.

3: Maybe that's it.

1: Kneady.

2: But without the 'k'.

Things I have lip read.

The following in sign performance.

VOICED: What a pity, their mouths say, she's

UNVOICED: deaf and dumb. And so pretty, too.
But at least she has her looks.
Some men like quiet.
Some men prefer women who are like Victorian children:
Seen, but not heard.
At least she won't nag.
At least she won't ask you what you're thinking when your mind's blank and you're watching TV.
And the phone bill will be small.

And she won't keep asking you if you love her.
And she won't always have the last word in an argument.
There'll be no shouting matches, no recriminations.
She'll keep herself to herself and be grateful.
And express herself by what she does.
After all, actions speak louder than words.

VOICED: Put like that, it's a pity more women aren't like her.

Transition:

I wonder sometimes about my fictional limbs – those phantom arms and legs, gracefully orbiting the earth in a disembodied ballet… limbing along in a parallel universe…

Walkie Talkies redux 1

I'm a lucky kind of person. I'm blessed a lot. I don't mean with the holy water at Lourdes (but believe me, I've had a narrow escape from a few of those outings.); I mean when people pass me on the street. There's a little cluck of the tongue and

'Bless, love her…'

There I am, exalted again.

And people always seem to think I've no money.

'The poor thing…Bless…'

Pitied and sanctified in one sentence; amazing. These walkie talkies must have very complicated emotional lives. But they're very generous. I was having a drink and a fag with some friends outside the pub the other day and this woman put some coins in my tin of Special Brew, and then got cross when I didn't have any stickers. 'Well, give me something,' she insisted and I said 'Sorry, love, I don't believe in charity. But thanks for the beer money. Next one's on you. Cheers.'

I hope my luck's with me, today. I've got my interview. They're all here: Mam and Dad, social worker, occupational therapist, director of the centre, the works. They think I'm daft, looking for the exit:

(As Mother.) 'Life's hard enough, why make it even more difficult?'

(As OT.) 'Everything's laid on here, you're well looked after.'

(As Mother.) 'What are you going to do, stuck on your own in a flat all day?'

I don't know. But I'd like the opportunity to find out.

I think the first thing I'd do is run a long, deep bath and float seductively in the bubbles. In water I'm weightless, like a mermaid – in my own element, free to move. I can't do that in here. They're scared I'll drown – in two inches of water, which is all they'll put in, despite my complaints. So, yes, float in the bath, be in my own element – away from watchful eyes and caring, prying fingers…

(As Mother.) 'You'll drown, I'm warning you. And living alone, you'll burn the place down. You'll get in a right mess.'

Perhaps. But like Gandhi said when arguing for Indian independence: at least it will be my mess.

Because it's my life.
Isn't it?

Retreat

Sometimes, sometimes I try to listen.

I sink down into my bones, my flesh, and imagine it like the texture of a peach – sweet and ripe, firm, ready for the picking. My inner organs, I mean.

The skin is an organ, the biggest in the body I'm told. Laid flat, it would cover the size of a football field – spread really, really thin.

But it's the inner organs.

The spleen and the liver and the bladder and the kidneys. The oesophagus. The lungs.

I all but forgot the heart.

The heart.

And I try to listen and sometimes I go even deeper, and imagine I can feel a thought forming – sense the electric impulse across the chemical soup between the neurons – feel that charge – the flicker of information from one cell to the next.

That's all it takes. One cell. That's what begins it all.

And I wonder if that's how it began over three billion years ago, the single-celled algae, ancestor of sponges and corals and trilobites. And the mosses and dinosaurs and flowers and ape-men; the dividing and sub-dividing, the multiplication of it all, of life.

Only mine was in the negative.

A cell has no morality. It doesn't know if it is good or bad. It is programmed solely to survive, to increase, to grow, expand. It has brute intelligence, like any expansionist force. It has tactics, surprise ambushes, invasions in unlikely places – a coup d'état that is secretive, silent, lethal, effective.

It's strange when your very being is a warzone carried out at molecular level. Visigoths and Genghis Khan – the slaughter in the trenches – massacre at Wounded Knee.

For this is what it is to be human, to be animal: to weaken, get sick; the slackening, the ebbing of strength, the indignity, the stripping of disease.

And I thought why me?

And I thought why not?

Why not me alongside the scarf wearing
women, defiant slash of war paint like blood
across their mouths; the men camouflaging
their catheters with shy smiles and draped
dressing-gowns, the spectre-thin children,
already haunting their parents' eyes.

Why not me as I sit with the others, a cup
of tea in our laps and bag of poison in
our veins, wondering how it can tell the
white hats from the black, wondering of
the innocent casualties through friendly
fire, sensing the singe of devastation,
the Blitzkrieg shock and awe, that fleshy
Dresden, wondering whose side is it on?

And for me the battle died down – just a
trace of smoke in my nostrils, a buzzing in
my blood, the taste of metal in my mouth
and the guilt of surviving.

Then nothing.

No D Day. No surrender. No peace treaty.
Just a retreat.

Final or temporary? No one knows.

So sometimes I find myself listening –
sinking down into the old territory, listening
for sniper fire, distant drums, for a sign just
one sign, a sign from one cell

that it will soon be all over.

Switch On, Switch Off. (After the Operation 1.)

Spoken and signed in theatricalised BSL or visual language.

A bilingual chorus.

1: *(English.)* It started with a desire to know what the wind sounded like

2: when it rattles, or roars, or whispers through the trees, like they say in books.

1: How can it do all those things?

3: Whistle

4: howl

5: screech

6: rustle…

1: How can one wind do so many things – or are there different winds?

3: Is this something you people know but I don't? Know the names and voices of different winds?

2: It *(in sign) feels (in English)* to me. It can be *(in sign) soft, silky, playful, chilly, rough, fresh.*

5: *(English.)* And what means *sound*, anyway?

1: I looked in a thesaurus. Sound.

(Signed and spoken, fast, distinct, but building to cacophony.)

5: Noise.

3: Resonance.

1&4: Hum. Echo. (Echo. Echo….)

2: Thud.

6&5&3: Reverberation.

4: Crash. Jingle.

6: Swish.

4: Clatter.

1: Ring.

2: Tinkle.

3: Jangle.

1-4: Drone. *(Sustained, as drone.)*

6: Murmur.

5: Buzz.

6: Whizz.

(Sudden swift recap of signs – unvoiced – huge, over-exaggerated signs using the whole body, ending in collapse.)

2: I was exhausted.

1: Did I really want to join this 'sound' world? How would you ever sleep?

4: Or work, read,

2: concentrate,

5: pass exams,

1: have a conversation with all that

ALL: *(Sign only)* bang whoosh whirr thump bang knock

1: *(English)* going on?

2: And did they really *sound* like that, or were they just ways of animating the mouth for lip reading?

1: For the first few days, after the operation, I did silly things

3: Switch on and off the light –

2: I never knew light had sound, before. It was short and quick and instant – maybe how it looked – dark and then light – dark and then light. Dark and then –

3: I stood in the hallway, the tip of my finger bloodless as I –

(Several demonstrate switching on and off a light switch: dark and then light; dark and then light; dark and then…)

5: And my cat. That strange

6: whatever you would call it.

4: I don't know what to call it.

6: You would know.

5: It's frightening, like my cat swallowed a bee.

1: And to speak like that is new: before, I didn't know bees *noised.*

(Shows sign for bee – then all copy – then start sign-interpreting the buzz: angry, dangerous – very different from smooth lovely bee sign.)

Boy Soldier

Nelson lost one eye and a limb.
Napoleon had one arm and he was little and probably epileptic. Joan of Arc is said now to have had migraines or petit mal. Some kind of seizures.

Almost all brilliant generals have been disabled.

An impairment gives you the edge, it means you have to work harder, but you've less to lose.
Fear is smaller.
Pain can be a frequent companion, not something to be warned with, or scared off from.
When you're in it and dealing with it, you become invincible.

I go to a regular school.
Not like my parents who, back in the olden

days – when everything was in black and white – back in the olden days my parents were considered special.
But not in a good sense.
They went to a special school where they learnt to play table football and say please and thank you and became very good at macramé.
Or so Dad says.
He pretends it's a joke, but I think he's bitter.
There's no need to be bitter when you can be strong.

Life isn't Disney channel.
I hate those programmes like 'Children's Hospital' where they use sick or disabled kids to pull at the heart strings.
There's always some boy with a shaved head
Mummy's brave little soldier –

Let me tell you about soldiers.
Let me tell you what soldiers endure.
They take pain and splintered bone and risk and fear and they eat it for breakfast.
That brave little soldier doesn't need your sympathy.

He's twice the man you'll ever be.

I'm Welsh.
At the Eisteddfod the Druid asks
'A oes heddwch?'
'Is there peace?'
There is not peace.
Fe godwn ni eto.
The campaign continues.

I'm a soldier.
I'm a general.
I've an army

And we know where you live.

JawJawJawJaw

Video of jawing mouths:

Jaw jaw jaw jaw jaw jaw. Teeth. Tongue. Cheeks. Lips.

Mouths are for kissing.

Your Tongue, My Lips

– Shiny buckles polished to a glint.
Leather. Stiff. Pliant, like skin.

– He called me doll face.

– The snap of strict leather, biting, the yawn of the corset's pink tongue across / my midriff, my nether, my body, my waist, tongue, my midriff, my nether, my body, my waist *(loops through next speech until 'ocean's depth //.')*

– Lower. Yes, there.
Ozone. Fingers trailing. Arch. Yes. Breath. Breath. Breathe. Breath. Pungent. The ache. The yearning. The salve. Sliding through the water, ocean's depth. //
The nibble of mouths. The slide the slip the ozone breath when your fingers are on in

– *(Simultaneous, from 'The nibble'.)* the yearning the heat the soldering touch the melt and ache the yawn the mouth blood-warm blood-rich

– Least of all my fingers

– open, the yielding, the meeting, the melting, the melding, the joining, the

– *(Simultaneous, from 'open'.)* My midriff, my nether, my body, my waist, tongue, my

– Come lie with me.
I'm all metal and pins.

– He called me doll face.
I hated dolls.
They took me to a child's psychologist for mutilating my toys, butchering my dolls, shortening their arms, their legs, their –

– Waist-high in the world.
Eye level, the crotch.
Well, that's handy, s/he said.

– I just wanted something that reflected me. In a world of bodies unlike my own, I wanted, as a child, something that looked like me.

– Can you do it? S/he asked.
I mean, have you the wherewithal?
The you know. Equipment.

– *(Low, simultaneously.)* The nibble of mouths. The slide. The slip. The ozone breath, when your fingers are on, in

– Is it all in working order? Shipshape?
Water tight? Ready for servicing?

– Everywhere there's men.

– Is it all in top notch working condition, or can't you?
What I mean is, can you do it?
You do have one, don't you?
Is it active?
Does it respond?
Does it work?

– 'It'

– Your todger. Dongle. Meat and two veg.
The family jewels.
Your sausage.
Love hammer.

Sex chisel.
Moan machine.

– I'm sorry.

– Love truncheon; trouser snake; light sabre; sword of Damacles; wanger; schlong; magic wand; cock-a-doodle-doo

– When I was a child I was told my front bottom was evil. It was a sinister place to be respected and feared and no one or nothing – least of all my fingers – should ever go there, or they'd be bitten off by the huge sharp teeth.

– I'm sorry.

– Your wotsit your thingy your

– Everywhere there's men.

On the bus, in the street, in cafes, on the tube, Cycling by in lycra, plums in a taut bag – fruit to be picked, squeezed, pressed against the mouth –

– But can you

– I'm dirty.

I'm very, very dirty –

– Sorry.   Sorry.

– – you need to take a shower after just thinking of me.

– Sorry.

– I like it best when it hurts.

– And with my body, made of pain

– it hurts all the time.

– So who's a lucky girl, then?

Transition:

I love my scars. I run my finger along them like braille reading my body, my history, reading the story of me.

Walkie Talkies redux 2

I'm a lucky kind of person. I'm blessed a lot. I don't mean with the holy water at Lourdes (but believe me, I've had a narrow escape from a few of those outings.); I mean when people pass me on the street. There's a little cluck of the tongue and

'Bless, love him…'

There I am, exalted again.

And people always seem to think I've no money.

'The poor thing… Bless…'

Pitied and sanctified in one sentence; amazing. These walkie talkies must have very complicated emotional lives. But they're very generous. I was having a drink and a fag with some friends outside the pub the other day and this bloke put some coins in my tin of Special Brew, and then got cross when I didn't have any stickers. 'Well, give me something,' he insisted and I said 'Sorry, butt, I don't believe in charity. But thanks for the beer money. Next one's on you. Cheers.'

I'd like that. A tattoo. They, of course, wouldn't hear of it.

'Not appropriate', they said.

For what? For me to spend my Disability Living Allowance on? It's my money. Or not appropriate for me, full stop?

It's my body.

Or so I like to think.

I fancy a great stonking Up Yours emblazoned on my chest. Not literally. I mean symbolically. Some beautiful, defiant symbol they'd look twice at when stripping me for a bath. I hate that, their jocular cheeriness. I know they're only trying to help and avoid embarrassment, spare my feelings, but I'm used to it and I like my privacy.

In water I'm weightless – in my own element, free to move. But they're scared I'll drown – in two inches of water, which is all they'll put in, despite my complaints.

But yes – something wonderful in hieroglyphics, or Chinese script, embroidered on my skin. Something only I would know the meaning of:

I Am Me.

Or: 100% concentrate.

Or Poison. Yes, Poison. I like that.

Act As If

1: Act as if nothing is wrong and you're fine.

2: Act as if they know something and might actually help you.

3: You think of the waste – all the taxpayer's money going for you to sit around in someone else's clothes, having a terrible time, not getting any better.

1: You should try harder.

3: You can't bear to think of all that money going to waste.

You've come here, you're taking up their valuable time, so you should tell them, tell them what the matter is.

2: You open your mouth and it comes out – is this what they want? Is the voice telling the right stories?

3: Is this what they need to fix what's wrong and make you better? Have you performed right? Given him all the right cues?

1: And then you realise it's just an ageing man with a cup of coffee gone cold beside him, who knows nothing. Like you, he's keeping up the pretence. Act as if. Once you both stop believing in his magic, his knowledge, it's just a man and a wo/man sitting in the interior of a room – unlived in, but pretending, like a film set – and it's never going to get better otherwise, so you try and make yourself believe.

2: Yes, doctor. Whatever you think is best, doctor.

3: And you're out in the corridor with a diagnosis and prescription for three types of sedatives in your hands.

1: But you know all this. You know the story. You've seen it in enough documentaries and mini-dramas on TV.

2: But what's different is the ease with which it can happen.

3: And to you.

Immediately following on into:

This is how madness begins.

1: This is how madness begins. Beautifully, but with euphoric pain.

2: This is how madness begins. With the smell of roses and Technicolor brightness and the surge of blood inside the veins.

3: This is how madness begins. With a couple of late nighters which extend into a week with no sleep, no change of clothing, no food, plenty of alcohol.

4: This is how madness begins. With a chemical imbalance formed in the womb.

5: This is how madness begins. With the death of a lover, the birth of a child, the last illness of a parent.

6: This is how madness begins. With the knowledge everything dies and therefore everything is utterly futile.

3: This is how madness begins. With clarity and understanding of the hidden truth in all things.

1: This is how madness begins.

Transition:

I wouldn't be in any other skin. I love this body. It works. It really, really works for me.

Beg.

We're supposed to crave contact.

I don't.

I like distance, space,

room around me to breathe.

I've been undressed too many times

– roughly –

not out of urgency, or eagerness – desire –

just rush.

Clothes yanked over my head. Buttons and flies undone

and I'm not even there.

They might as well be undressing a corpse

– solid air –

they don't see me.

They might even be chatting to someone in another room and I'm just a chore,

an entity to be stripped, examined, washed, dressed, or put to bed.

That's why you're not allowed to touch me.

You may crave it

You might even beg.

So go on then: beg.

Beg. Beg for me.

Beg.

You know you'd never experience anything else quite like it.

No one else quite like me.

So go on.

I know you want to.

I can see your eyes.

Go on:

Beg.

Chorus.

Performed chorally, first in BSL/visual language, second, in English/ spoken language:

Chorus: Thank you so, so much for patronising me and denying me my human rights. You're absolutely right, why would I need civil liberties? I don't need to work, to contribute, to be independent, part of society, social life. Yes, we are fire hazards, and such an expensive drain with our demands for ramps, and equality, and access to work and public buildings like schools and nightclubs, supermarkets and cinemas. The politicians are right; we shouldn't be left to fester. Make those cuts and save the taxpayers money. Put us back behind the walls, into the homes, the families, the institutions. Make us invisible again and we'll just be grateful.

Transition:

Joy.

Joyous.

Joyful.

Full of joy.

Filled with it.

Joy.

Joy.

Luvvies

1: I'm always playing zombies.

2: The sick and twisted psycho.

1: I suppose it's better than being one of the Magnificent 7 – and I'm talking Snow White here, not Yul Brynner. What I'd give to be 'Woman 1'. That's it, just 'Woman 1'.

2: Or 'Neighbour 3'… 'Fish and chip customer' on *EastEnders*…

1: Even 'Waiting Patient' in *Holby City* – you know, some poor love with a makeshift bandage over their eye… But – no…

2: No…

1: No bit part for me. I always have to be the star attraction.

2: The ghoulish complication that has the doctors scratching their heads or each others' eyes out.

1: Whether it's a horror flick or not, I'm always the monster.

The experiment gone horribly wrong.

2: The accident people flinch at when first meeting.

1: The misunderstood evil genius, just wanting a bit of love.

2: Or my personal favourite: the plot device.

1: I did a 'crip' cameo on a cop show the other week, leading a demonstration about the pig pen not being fully accessible.

2: Storylined by a wheelchair-using writer on an equal opps, inclusive, cultural diversity attachment, by any chance?

1: Got it in one…
My character was protesting it was every disabled person's right to be treated like a criminal. Fantastic. I smashed a few windows, broke the peace, was arrested for assaulting a WPC and then proved my point, as they couldn't take me down into the cells because of the stairs.

2: That must've been nice, playing a human.

1: Yeah. I hadn't done that since a mini-series for the Beeb to commemorate the 90th anniversary of the First World War. I was playing an ambulance driver on the Front who went over a landmine… .

2: You get the picture.

1: Typecast again.

Transition

I wouldn't be in any other skin. I love this body. It works. It really, really works for me.

After the Operation (2).

In spoken and visual language:

(Spoken) 'You're jumpy,' my girlfriend said and we both jumped, me at the sudden noise, and her at the shock of being heard. 'I keep forgetting you can hear me,' she said, her voice still a surprise, and *(signed) still a disappointment. (Spoken)* it's *(signed) thin and weak and flat (spoken)* and I expected *(signed) full and rich and musical and beautiful.*
(Spoken) 'I never had you down as the neurotic type',
She'd never used that tone of face with me, before.
'You used to be better than diazepam; a happy pill on legs. It was your *(signed and spoken)* U.S.P. *(spoken)* and what attracted me to you in the first place.'

I haven't been able to sleep well since the operation.
I lie awake in bed. Before, I would dream – slide into sleep like *(signed and spoken)* getting into *a bath of warm water* all *(signed) dreaming, smiling, relaxed…*
In water I'm weightless,
(signed) like a mermaid – in my own element, free to move.
(Spoken) Now *(signed) I lie awake, wide eyed, in terror*

(spoken) hearing *(signed) robbers… ghosts… wild animals with big teeth (spoken)* waiting to be slaughtered in my bed.
I wish the doctor had warned me.
Sound ambushes.
(Visual and spoken language.) It creeps up and taps my shoulder like the children's game Grandmother's Footsteps. It pounces, close to the ear; it bounces screaming out of the doorbell, or the phone, or a once gently vibrating alarm clock. It tweets like a chatty budgie when the batteries on the fire alarm are low, comes yelling round corners, jetting across the sky, roaring down the road and I'm cautious and nervous, waiting for the next attack.
(Spoken) I liked it better when my house didn't groan.
I liked my home when it was silent bricks and mortar, before it started to complain.
And then just as I'm *(signed and spoken) dropping off to sleep – I'm woken again* – by my blood itself, pulsing *(spoken only)* my blood pulsing through my ear as I rest my head on the pillow – ticking – it sounds like my body's *ticking* – the winding down mechanism of life itself.
Sound makes you aware of your mortality.
You can hear that doomsday clock in your blood.
'You're getting morbid,' my girlfriend said.

I've decided hearing is existential.

A Short History of Fear

I speak to you, the useless eaters, the mongs, the spazzies, the shunned, the feared, those with differently-abled limbs, minds, organs, senses, those intellectually challenged by hate and prejudice, not by brain circuitry. The schitzos, the deafies, the crippled, the mad, bad, and dangerous to know – I salute you – for by your existence you threaten the narrow definition of human variety, you broaden the scope of homo-sapien possibilities, you challenge normalcy, the normative, Norm – and he hates you for it. You, with the Stevie Wonder eyes, the Parkinson's touch, the FDR shuffle and shake, your tush proud and in that chair – let us carry you aloft in your chariot, you marvel, you scientific enigma, you medical conundrum, you gem of the genome. O glorious freak of nature, let us cherish you and lay tribute at your miraculous twisted feet, you brittle beauty, boned like a Fabergé egg, precious one, unique.

You threatened, endangered species, let us save you for future generations, you rare jewel of genetic code, dodo diamond of DNA.

Do you know, even for one moment, how extraordinary you are? You are the wonders of the past, the Cyclops, the Minotaur – no wonder they feared you, with your capacity to be beyond what they could ever be, just by breathing.

You are the dragon of their folklore, the bogeyman of their chastising tales. No wonder they set out on crusades to destroy you – or, in later years, paid for the privilege to see you eat, walk, sleep, cry, turn your gorgon eye towards them, your own limbs already petrified, manacled to the walls in the dungeons of their asylums. No wonder they queued to watch you swallow down their disabling pills and pushed for front row seats at the performance of your lobotomy, you sedated but still awake, wide-eyed at the stab of the stiletto into your brain via an eye socket, this their brutal attempt to subdue your visions and appetites.

You, whose exquisite hands sculpt meaning into air, defying gravity and the root of all Indo-European languages: How they hate you for your visceral eloquence and synapse-firing brain so different from their own lit up language centres. No wonder they tried to destroy you and deny your existence, force your mouth to shape as theirs, stamp on your culture and language as they tied your tongue behind your back.

I speak to you, the rewired, reformed, resuscitated, you 6 million dollared men and women, they now have the technology to rebuild you, but they will never surpass your audacious evolution. You are both historic and forthcoming, the monstered past and the cyborg future, O Darth Vader of their nights and dreams, you who breathe water and have oxygen piped to your lungs, you molecular marvel who inhale pharmaceuticals and cough out spume, you amaze me. I am dazzled. I salute you all, you definitive shock and awe, you mercurial mutants, you species who both prove and disprove Darwin – long may you continue, long may you thrive.

No wonder they feared you.

End.

the 9 Fridas

Notes

This performance text is a mosaic, with many representations of Frida Kahlo, and monologues delivered by specifically non-Frida figures/characters (1 – 4.) that tell contemporary stories paralleling aspects of her biography as F journeys through memory and the Mayan afterlife.

There are other representations of Frida: puppets, dolls, iconography. The monologues titled 'Individual comments on her art no.1 – 7' refer to specific paintings, which I have indicated but would prefer not to be seen in production, so we listen to the audio description of her work, but never see it.

Some monologues are mediatised, with the optional pre-set – a recorded discussion of her art as if from an arts review radio programme.

The action is continuous and ever-changing in form and style.

This text reproduces the assignment of lines and parts for the original Taiwanese cast of five actors (numbered 1 – 4, plus F). 1– 4 double up and play different personas as well as the chorus accompanying F on her journey through the Mayan Underworld. It is only F who remains the same throughout – s/he is but is not Frida Kahlo, as are all.

It could have a larger live cast, reassigning lines accordingly.

The cast is a mix of male and female, hearing and Deaf, disabled and non-disabled performers, but all dressed as Frida Kahlo from her portraits and paintings – some in her famous Tehuana regional Mexican dress, others in her western clothes – Levi's 501 jeans, overalls, a three-piece suit, and so on – and various corsets – some orthopedic, others lingerie.

I imagine a constant dressing and redressing of the cast – constantly moving and creating still images of her self-portraiture, but also preparing vegetables and flowers in still life arrangements/kitchen scenarios preparing a fiesta.

Much of the stage business will be about creating the final image – that of a traditional ofrenda – an altar to the deceased.

the 9 fridas: world premiere in Mandarin (translation by Betty Chen) on invitation of Taipei Arts Festival 2014 (Yi-Wei Keng, Artistic Director).

Produced by Mobius Strip Theatre (Taipei); Faye Leung, Alex Cheung (Co-Artistic Directors); Cordelia Yang (Executive Producer, Company Manager) in association with Hong Kong Repertory Theatre.

Cast (on-stage ensemble)

F	Faye Leung
1	Po-Ting Chen
2	Chih-Chung Cheng
3	Ying-Hsuan Hsieh
4	Wai Hang Rocelia Fung
5	Alex Cheung

Video Cast	Lin Chien-Lang
	Ying-Ni Ma
	Pun Hui-Yun Chen

Spanish translation and voice-over

Victor Ramirez Ladron De Guevara

Director	Phillip Zarrilli
Costume Design	YS Lee
Set Design	Yy Lim
Lighting Design	Fung Kwok Kee Gabriel
Music Design	Nicolas Saito
Video Design	Alex Cheung
Stage Manager	Min-Tzu Liao

OPTIONAL PRESET

A cultural radio programme: a recording of many voices in discussion as the audience comes in – overlapping, disagreeing… The lines assigned to specific voices here reproduces the original production, but can be reassigned for different sized casts.

7: We're broadcasting from the opening of a major art exhibition – the first time this world famous Mexican artist's work has been seen in the city. I'm joined by a panel of experts to discuss her paintings and the controversial artist's reputation….

1: She is the ultimate example of tragic but brave…

2: I disagree.

3: Oh come on, her heroic suffering becomes part of her art.

5: It's her 'wounded and weeping' that gets me.

2: But she's not asking for pity – it's not maudlin, or sentimental – there's always this intense dignity.

4: She frightens me. I don't like it.

2: That's because she's challenging your idea of selfhood with her deconstruction of dominant notions of body-self and normalcy.

4: No: I don't like it because there's blood and suffering and it's all about pain.

1: She creates an iconography of her own body, with repeated recognisable features – her hair, that monobrow, the challenging scrutiny of the viewer –

2: She's questioning the power relationships between men and women, between developed and developing nations, between the histories and belief systems of old and new, east and west.

6: She understands. She just gets it.

7: Okay, we're talking about the Broken Column – painted in 1944 soon after surgery when she was confined, rather as in 1927, in this particular kind of – what? Orthopedic corset –

4: It's passive aggression.

2: She's confined – the desert behind. Tears dot her cheeks and these little tacks or nails are piercing her naked body, which is split in two, with a broken –

7: – Her spine is replaced by this broken, shattered ancient Greek column, and her whole torso is held together with the aforementioned orthopedic corset.

8: Well it's clearly a metaphor, isn't it? The phallus, the pain of sex.

2: It clearly symbolises the restrictions of physical disability – of a patient – mere meat – restricted within the medical model of

5: Let's just describe the painting, shall we?

1: It's as though the doctor she wished to be before the accident remains and does surgery on herself; this anatomically precise representation of the inner – as though she could remove her skin and flesh and display the heart, the foetus, the broken spinal column –

7: It recalls the brutal way she was pierced by a metal handrail, in through the side, out through the vagina –

5: Can we put aside this tyranny of biography and focus on the art?

3: But the art IS her biography – she made art from her life, so it's pertinent.

9: In the painting that wound in the side, of course, brings up Christ

2: No it doesn't. She was an intellectual and a revolutionary, the cadre and lover of Trotsky, who in her youth read Nietzsche, Schopenhauer, Hegel, Marx –

9: – even the white hospital sheet around her hips suggests the winding sheet – Christ risen from the

2: She was a Stalinist, an atheist –

6: She's just a woman, just like me.

7: Which is the ultimate story of capitalism, of course – the self-professed communist still nothing without the steel and medical advances of America, the modernism of Detroit –

9: She's a Mexican saint, bristling with arrows, displaying her suffering – physical and spiritual.

7: – the salvation of capitalism.

4: Look: it's a desert landscape and a crying naked woman smashed to smithereens just about holding it together, full of steel and nails and tears rolling down her cheeks and it's depressing! It's disturbing! It's –

Immediately into live text of:

1.

Individual comments on her paintings no. 1

(Various photographs by Nikolas Murray.)

F: She is everywhere. A woman with flowers in her hair. A woman with a lipsticked mouth like a bleeding wound. A woman whose whole body is a wound. Wounded. Wounding in the even eyed stare out from the picture frame. Steady. Wielding an emotional machete, necklaced with the barbed wire of truth: This is how the body hurts. This is pain. This is what the body endures.

A woman with an abundance of flowers in her hair. Her own muse, her own model, her own means of production, her own self.

Continuous action, transition into:

2.

Title projected: THE WOULD BE MOTHER

A tight spotlight on 3's face. Alone.

The other faces become lit as they speak.

The scene begins solitary and ends collective.

3: He pulls me out of sleep, like a deep sea trawler – that slow motion haul – and I'm pulled along, fingers caught in the net, the mesh pressing against my neck, trawled through the water, the prickly fibres of the rope cutting into my throat, the bend in my leg – half in, half out – limbs floating free outside the net, body caught against the rope, trawled backwards against the current, and I'm drowning, it just occurs to me I'm drowning, drawn through the water in a slow motion drag – and it's him driving this, it's him trawling, it's him pulling me up from sleep and I wake with a gasp, like my head breaking the surface. I come up and alert, dragged from the depths, blinking, heart beating, air in my mouth, listening. Was that his cry? Is that him awake? Is he hungry, needing me, wanting the warmth and nurture of my body – is that him calling for me, a cry to haul me through the depths

1: of demerol

4: of morphine

F: of tequila

2: of marijuana

F: of opium

3: of forgetting but not forgetting?

And I remember. I'm called by the potential of something that has never been. He was never born. He never formed fingernails, or spleen, or lungs worthy of air. He only ever swam in my waters before being hauled out, expelled from the salty waters of my uterus, trawled out too soon. And because of his not being, his not hereness, I'm woken and I think of this useless harbour, this worthless vessel, this broken column that refuses to sustain life. And I wonder: What's the use and purpose of me at all?

All figures visible. A change:

3.

All figures form a collective tableau of Kahlo's individual self-portraits. They stare out at the audience, then break the tableau with:

1: Shall we begin: tell it?

F: I'm so tired of telling, I'm forgetting how it all went.

4: Is that part of the process? Forgetfulness?

3: I see it as a kindness. If we remembered, how could we bear it all?

1: First you dismember, then you remember:

2: The anatomy of art. Like the artists of the Renaissance copying cadavers on the slab: a study of the passions of Christ, the beheading of St John,

3: – the foetus in formaldehyde.

F: So you want to start telling from there?
The hospital in Detroit – my stillborn baby floating like a kite above my head, attached to me by a red ribbon as I lie naked, weeping, on the bed.

3: Must you really?

4: You said forgetfulness was a kindness.

3: This…relishing morbidity. The constant parading of yourself – bleeding, broken, crying –

F: What did you expect me to paint? Tulips in a vase?

2: Staring.

1: Yes. Mustn't forget the staring.

They all take staring tableaux, sustaining them throughout the following

Always staring straight out at the viewer

2: if they dare look.

4: And don't flinch.

They stare out at the audience. The staring tableaux ends

F: I find it comforting. Serene, almost.

4: You've never been serene.

Always screaming, always singing, telling bawdy jokes, upstaging the American blondes with their minks and their money and perfect legs and unscarred bodies –

1: Calling with the siren song of sex,

2: Of magnificence,

3: Of filth.

F: Hold your friends close and your enemies even closer.

3: But you're not the only woman disaster happened to.

4: You're not the first to have been betrayed, or hurt

3: or lost a baby

1: or reinvented herself.

2: You're not the first woman to be disabled.

F: Is that why you're here?

1: Once upon a time there was a little girl of mixed cultural heritage who caught polio aged six, and survived.

4: Once upon a time there was a woman who divorced, forgave, then remarried her faithless husband.

3: Once upon a time there was a would-be mother who miscarried and miscarried and who could never carry her baby full term.

4: Once upon a time there was a little damaged wife who became a world-famous artist.

F: Once upon a time there was a

(Beat.)

I paint my reality so they cannot contain me. I paint my reality so they will love me.
I paint what I know

1: Joy

2: Pain

4: Betrayal

F I paint my reality so they will not forget me.

A change.

Making up, 'painting' themselves.

1: First, the preparation. The priming of the canvas.

F: Some vermillion.

3: Brows, dark.

4: Arched like a bird flying away.

F: Little moustache.

2: They like that.

F: A little female, a little male, a bit of both, what's under the skirt?

2: Nothing but Frida Peg leg with her sawn-off phantom limb.

F: 'Like a skellington in its wellingtons.'

I flaunt my alegra the way a peacock spreads its tail – display as camouflage. A conjuror's trick. Smoke and mirrors. Now you see me, now you see me even more…

Immediately into solo:

4.

Title projected: THE BEAUTY TERRORIST: A WOMAN'S HEAD ON A LION'S BODY

2: I have been terrorised by beauty all my life.
I haven't a pretty face – I know that. And it's fine.
My body's… well, it's not the kind you see in the Style pages of the Sunday papers, let's put it that way.
I see this ideal on every magazine cover, in every wannabe contorting her body, shape-shifting – but not in a good way. All those breathing Barbies, or the stick-thin lolliop heads – wanting to be special, to stand out from the herd in some way…
Moo.
My body's different. Puzzling, maybe.
My silhouette strays from the expected shape.
The shadow I throw isn't straightforwardly beguiling. My body's an enigma.
And I love it.
I'm a sphinx – a woman's head on a lion's body.
I want to stare out at those poor norms with their predictable bodies and their predictable attitudes and go 'I know you're looking. You may pretend you didn't double-take, but I saw that little sag, the tiny drop in your jaw when you rubber necked to get another glimpse of me. What, has the circus come to town?'
And raise my chin and relish it.
And give them That Stare.

I wasn't always like this.
Confident.
I used to be a little mouse who would scuttle home and weep over the cheese parings at the smallest slight.
'Oh, I'm different. Poor me. Boo-hoo.'
Doing my best to keep it all tidy and tucked away. Don't show.
Aspire to invisibility with your funny legs and your twisted back
and unlikely hips.
But that was before.
Now I want to flaunt my body the way a peacock displays its tail.
And it's all down to her.
Scars are not usually beautiful, but she has made mine so.
I am decked out in scars, like constellations, the Milky Way.

WE SEE THE STARS.

5.

They look up at the stars, trace constellations.

SPEAKER may be mediatised, pre-filmed, projected on a screen.

SPEAKER: In Mayan myth, the heavens, the Road to Xibalbá, was represented by the dark rift visible in the Milky Way. Yax'ché, the world tree, is at the centre of The World, and grows through the 9 Underworld levels. Each level has its own ruler, but Mitnal, the lowest level, is the most terrible of the 9 hells of the underworld, for here everybody suffers, being ruled by the skeleton Death God, Ah Puch.

1: Le pelona, death. Her companion through life.

F: Is that where I am? The lowest of the 9 hells, where everybody suffers…? For we do. We put a good face on it, lipstick on the sugar skull, but we suffer.

1: It's all part of the process.

3: The letting go

2: The moving on

4: The taking leave

1: The dying.

F: Am I dying?

(Beat.)

I thought I was already dead.

I'm dead. Aren't I?

It's over, surely?

Am I not done yet?

2: All except the last journey.

4: You know the way.

3: But you will always live on in your art.

F: Such clichés are the very substance of hell.

1: The 9 hells through which you pass, Friducha.

SPEAKER: In the realm of Xibalba, the K'iche Shades, the place of fear. Passing through the house of ghosts, through the 9 houses of the underworld.

F: Where I am is where I have always been.
A place of the living, a place of the dead.

Transition, audio in Spanish. An extract from Frida's journal:

'Espejo de la noche.

Tus ojos, espadas verdes dentro de mi carne, ondas entre nuestras manos.

Todo tú en un espacio lleno de sonidos – en la sombra y en la luz. Te llaman Auxochrome, el que quién captura el color. Yo cromóforo – el que quién da el color….Tu palabra viaja la totalidad de espacio hasta llegar a mis células, que son estrellas, y alcanza las tuyas que son mi luz.

Fantasmas. '

['Mirror of the night.
Your eyes green swords inside my flesh,
waves between our hands.

All of you in a space full of sounds – in the shade and in the light. You are called Auxochrome the one who captures colour. I chromophore – the one who gives colour..... Your word travels the entirety of space and reaches my cells which are my stars then goes to yours which are my light.
Ghosts.']

6.

Individual statements about her art no. 2

(Self portrait with Dr Farrell.)

2: I'd never seen a woman in a wheelchair in a painting, before. Naked, stretched on a bed, yes, or drowning in the river, yes, but sitting in a wheelchair looking out at me?
And not only that, but before the easel in an outfit like an artist's smock, with brushes and paint and a palette shaped like a heart in her hand.
The artist. The creator. As well as the muse.
But the wheel of the chair is not hidden. It's an equal part of the composition, with the handle for pushing clearly visible at her shoulder blade.
And no shame.
That's what got me when I realised. It's not hidden. And there's no apology, or embarrassment, just fact.
I can be whole and in control and an artist even with polio, with spina bifida, even with a missing limb. And there's no shame.

Immediately into:

7.

F: Cuatezona of my heart, this is too sombre. We need some tequila! Music!

F plays hostess – she mingles, dances, and pours drinks, interacting with the audience or invisible guests at her 'party'.

The others watch on, gossiping. Music plays – F dances – the others watch and gossip.

3: She's made art out of attitude – this glorious mirage from very rickety raw materials indeed.

2: That's the artist in her, knowing of appearances, the power of image.

3: I think she's more of a technician, that knowledge of good lighting, throwing shadows and directing our gaze exactly to where she wants it to be.

1: On her.

3: It's like she doesn't exist unless we're staring at her.

2: Or she at us.

F: It doesn't matter they cut off my leg, I levitate.

1: She's a mirrorball.

4: Cracked?

1: Made of multiple, shiny, sharp, pointed pieces. No substance, just reflecting back what's around.

2: And you think to do that doesn't take genius?

4: Or substance?

3: Psychologists claim she's a raging narcissist, a liar – with a mass of operations she didn't really need.

2: Really?

3: So they say.

F: You don't believe I've lost a paw? Come look at my red leather boots, with the golden bells…

3: Along with having an addictive personality, she's an obsessive attention-seeker.

F: Oh, no – hidden by the skirts… You'll have to go under…

4: He was as bad, her husband – they were both notorious – communists and bohemians. He was the most famous artist in the world –

F: You don't want to play with Frida wooden leg of Coyosan of the coyotes?

4: – and some kind of erotic maniac.

3: There was legendary infidelity on both sides.

F: Give your darling Friducha one kiss. It doesn't matter if you're a boy, a girl, neither, or both, I don't mind.

3: He couldn't pass anything female – including her sister – without first trying to have sex. And I mean anything female. Species wasn't important.

F: No no, I won't force you. I don't want to look like a son of a b.b.com[13] in your lovely eyes…

2: This need to be visible, it's a fear of being forgotten: This continual search for affirmation, love. It's low self-esteem.

F steals a kiss.

F: You may cut off these limbs but you'll not stop this skeleton from dancing. 'Why do I need feet when I have wings to fly?'

2 approaches her.

2: *(to F.)* Why do you think you're second best?

F: *(to 2.)* I don't.

2: Then why do you try so hard?

Immediately into solo:

8.

Title projected: THE REPLACEMENT FOR THE IRREPLACABLE

1: You doubt, sometimes, if you're actually loved. It's the hesitation in a smile – barely noticeable – just a little frown: 'Oh. You're not quite whom I expected, but you'll do' – and then the corners of the lips lift. But before that there's a slight delay – disappointment in the eyes – and then it disappears as though it never was, but you felt it.

13 Or utilize Kahlo's own 'son of a bi…shop.'

You feel it. And you can never live up to the expectation of that first, longed-for son who died and whom your parents made you to replace.

4: The first disappointment is your gender. And no matter how much you cross dress, or are photographed in three-piece suits with your hair slicked back, cane held as a dandy between your fingers, you're still female and everyone knows what's missing beneath the buttoned flies of that good wool suit.

1: And no matter how clever you are, nor how many languages you speak, or German philosophers you can quote by heart, you're still not him.
And so you join the line of psychologically damaged 'Replacement Children' –

4: – Vincent van Gogh, Salvador Dali –

1: – who can never, despite their brilliance and prolific over– achieving gain that approval, that self-worth.

4: You can't compete with memory, a corpse.

1: The second disappointment is the demands of your body and the piles of hospital bills, the needed treatment too expensive to have. That brings with it the disappointment of your disability, the fixable body unfixed owing to lack of funds.

4: But you smile and pretend it doesn't matter,

1: for it doesn't

4: for you're not the longed-for son and heir.

1: You're just another daughter

4: yet another girl.

9.

Projection: HOW TO BE A GOOD WIFE

A puppet show or playing with dolls representing Frida, her regional dress and various forms of Mexicana – the embroidered napkins, the colourful woven basket, etc. A transformation from modern, urban dress into the long layered Tehuana dress from the Oaxaca region of Mexico – hair is plaited and pinned up. The process is then reversed during scene 10.

VOICE A: Dress solely for his pleasure. Dress only for your man, regardless of your comfort, aesthetic, or previous style: Enter the country bumpkin in her staid shapeless traditional wear, heavy on the embroidery. The exotic peasant in a blouse bought from any farmer's market, topped with cheap beads and priceless pre-Columbian jade.

VOICE B: The way to a man's heart is through his sternum with an oscillating saw powered by electricity.
Sorry:
The way to a man's heart is through his stomach. Lunchtime becomes a pageant – the flower-festooned basket filled with favourite traditional fare taking the whole morning to cook; napkins embroidered with 'I adore you' – the wife/maid bringing lunch to her king. The more public these signs of sublimation, the more surrendered the wife, the better.

VOICE C: Be understanding when he strays. You may feel he is a god, but he's only human and there's only one of him, with a limited mortal life span, so don't be greedy and selfish – be generous. You can't have him to yourself. Lions in their pride are not monogamous. Learn to share – but be faithful yourself.

10.

Projected title: THE LONG HAIRED WIFE LISTENING TO THE RADIO

Tight focus on 4

4: I was listening to the radio. Well, it was on – I wasn't really paying attention – I just wanted some background noise, some thing to break the silence as I waited. For him. Pretending. Not to be waiting. But waiting. For him. They were playing carols on the radio. Those choirboys made my head ache – and the announcer said somewhere on the earth it was snowing. Not here, naturally, but somewhere. Some where there was snow. Which would be nice. Snow. Snowing. I was walking and sitting with the radio on in the background somewhere. Just walking from one room to another, waiting, but not waiting, sitting, getting up, looking at things. Nothing in particular. Just things. Some things he'd given me. Others I'd just sort of acquired. Strange how we do that. Start out with nothing and somehow just. Acquire. Things. And they weigh you down. And I remembered a dinner party once somewhere in another city with this musician, a fellow guest, a musician who was Jewish who said suddenly and a propos nothing she always carried her passport with her in case she needed to leave the country suddenly. And by the door at her home she had a small valise – that's the word she used, quite old fashioned, valise – a small valise filled with essentials, packed and ready. 'I could just pick it up and go somewhere else at a moment's notice and begin a new life,' she said 'when the need arose' and it struck me. Not just the 'when' instead of 'if'. Not just the fear she lived under, this constant threat she perceived for possible imminent persecution and the need for flight, but the lightness. This extraordinary lightness she had compared to the weight of things that held me in place. Like a stone. And I wanted to breathe and you know how it does, sometimes, it catches – my breath caught

and I had to almost struggle, gulp down the air, my shoulders lifting, constricted in my chest by the weight of my lungs, those objects, this – waiting.
And so I picked up the scissors and cut off my hair.
Not at the dinner party, of course. Later. In my rooms, drifting from one to another, waiting, walking, not really listening to the radio when somewhere on the earth the snow settled. And with each snip I grew giddy. It makes an extraordinary noise, the slow motion slicing together of the blades. And the hair follicle.
Each strand, a delicate but definite severing. Slice. Slide. Sever. And so I did my wrists. Or was just about to. When he walked in. And he saw me there, dressed in his clothes because they smelt of him, dressed in his suit so I could feel him surround me and he saw the long long strands of my long long hair which he loved so much, severed. And even then I could smell her on him.

A shift, but still continuous action.

Into:

11.

4: If I could understand.
I have to – He
and she

F & 4: my sister, my almost twin, my childhood friend

F: my

4: He

Projection: FRIDA'S FIESTAS: DEAD MAN'S BREAD.

Mediatised Cooking Frida (F2.) begins instruction on how to make Dead Man's Bread for Day of the Dead feasting, using Kahlo's actual recipe.

F2: Mound one kilo of flour onto your counter and make a well in the centre. Place 400g of sugar, two tablespoons of butter, some active yeast, two teaspoons of cinnamon, a generous splash of vanilla extract and 125ml of milk in the well and work into a dough.

4: It would have been his idea. I know him. And I know she's not capable of
I know her
I thought I
Double betrayal.
It's like smashed

F2: Combine all the ingredients and work into a dough.

4: Like they slipped their fingers in under my ribs, unhooked my breastbone, opened my ribcage and took my fluttering heart, little bird, they took it from within its protective cage

F2: Knead the dough vigorously. If there has been anyone irritating you lately, well, get to work on the dough: it's them.

4: they soothed me, made me trust – I trusted them – I relaxed enough for them to jemmy open my ribs, make the safe unsafe, take out the bleeding heart and smash it – pulverise it – they mashed it to pulp between their cheating careless faithless hands.
Not unfaithful.
Faithless.

F2: Shape into a ball, grease and flour, then leave in a warm place until doubled in size.

4: Traitors.

F: Worse, killers.

4: They've murdered my trust, they've slaughtered my heart.

F2: Cover with a towel and refrigerate overnight.

F & 4: I need to know why.

F2: Next morning – sun is up, all is well –

4: Such violence.

F2: Shape the dough into balls the size of a peach. Decorate with strips of rolled dough to look like bones and leave them to rise in a warm place.

4: Did they think I'd not know?

F2: Then dust with sugar, and bake in a preheated oven, 175 degrees, for thirty minutes or until the bottoms sound hollow when tapped, just like dead man's bread, which this is.

Cooking ends.

Confidantes, sharing stories of their unfaithful men

4: Did they think I'd not find out?
She who has never been able to keep a secret from me, never.

F: He can't keep the identity of his latest conquests quiet, but must come and brag, drag the victim in like a tomcat in the night, parading the decapitated bird on my bed.

3: I made myself his confidante, thinking this was a way I could keep the tie between us.

F: He would confess and we would laugh, the smoke from my cigarette in my throat, the whiskey burning like acid.

3: I pretended to be amused – I encouraged him, just to try and keep him.

F: An open marriage. Progressive. Contemporary.

3: We weren't going to be bourgeois, or suburban. No one had ever loved like us before; everything else was just sex. It didn't mean anything.

F: This freedom more binding and cutting than piano wire.

4: He's a child, like a boy with his catapult wanting to show the prize he has killed.
Only this time it was me.

3: We know things, we women who do not sleep, but press an ear to the pillow, hearing the constant lurch of the heart. We who pretend to take sleeping pills but sick them up, who have doubts and inklings if not actual names, dates, and times. We who register an unfamiliar perfume, a mysterious credit card bill, a receipt for lingerie never received, a hotel meal never shared; who listen for the silent midnight phone calls, the texts deleted, who clock his absent minutes in the garden, when putting the bins out, doing the recycling, walking the dog. We the cheated women who add up the lax unaccounted for minutes, and find a lifetime in the balance.

2: And so you become one of those crying women measuring out hours with glasses of 'anything but chardonnay' and stolen cigarettes.

F: She who pays more attention to her appearance

4: or suddenly none at all, dragging yourself round in a ratty towelling dressing gown, sleeping in someone else's clothes because they smell of them, clutching valentine mementoes

F: or, more usually, a half bottle of vodka

1: looking like shit

2: like an abandoned house, half lived in, place for cats to rut or hide away in and die.

4: And so you become careless or too watchful, sitting on the stairs, belly on fire for him, wanting him there, thinking he will know, thinking he will come, thinking he will answer your silent call done without the use of technology, just by sheer concentration.

2: And does he come?

Beat. They don't dare look at each other.

F: Hold your friends close and your enemies even closer. Make pacts with the ex-wives and deserted mistresses, befriend the plumped-up, wide-eyed future hopefuls, those able to open shapely legs and receive. Your competition: Those who lost virginities through natural ways, not from inanimate objects driven by the volition of speed, of accident, of the gods, of unseen forces, of the energy of life, of the universe itself.

4: Love.

They laugh.

Immediately into:

12.

Projection: THE BI-CURIOUS LOVER

1: And I do and I love you for you are me. Your chromosomes and photons and nuclei are mine. I am made of you and you are the universe, the stars in the lane in the dark, the sodium streetlights in the city are you, the phosphorous in the sea, each tiny speck of tiny sand particles that make up where the sea meets the land are you, just as the salt that makes the oceans is.

And you are my breath, the O2 in my blood, the air in my lungs, the smile on my lips, the tongue in my mouth, the body in my bed, I want you, for us to merge like a venn diagram, you balance me like a fraction, an equation, a well-made sum. I want to dissolve like the sugar in your tea and have you smack your lips and drink me all up, consume me, so I am part of you, inside. We are one and constitute the unknown universe.

I want to go shopping and buy you underwear, toothpaste, and non-allergen products without parabens and deodorant which hasn't been rubbed in the eyes of rabbits or injected into mice. And to soothe ayervedic oils into your skin and make you lemsip when you sneeze and put my hand to your forehead when you run a fever and knit you jumpers for when it's cold. I want to walk beside you down the street and rest my hand on yours in the cinema and watch not the screen but your face.

You are my own personal pandemic, my bird flu, my SARS. You have infected me and there's no cure but to keep loving you, despite the side effects. And although it hurts me and although you inflict this pain

I can never be without you and I am grateful.

13.

Individual responses to her art no.3

(Portrait of Lucha Maria, a girl from Tehuacan.)

4: She sits alone on her rock on the Street of Death, between the pyramids of the sun and the moon in Teotihuacan, the city of the gods. El sol, the sun, is descending to incinerate us all, ungrateful humans, slow with our blood offerings.
And I looked at the painting and I knew then: I won't sacrifice myself to your brilliance, though you scald me, you burn me up. I will aim at the stars, at the hare in the moon, and fly off alone in my camouflage plane.

WE SEE THE STARS

14.

Change. Choral. A re-set.

1: Shall we begin again: tell it?

F: I'm so tired of telling, I'm forgetting how it all went. Is that possible? Part of the process? Forgetfulness?

3: The letting go

2: The moving on

4: The taking leave

F: Am I not done yet?

Mediatised speaker

SPEAKER: I am following the dark rift visible in the Milky Way, through the 9 Underworld levels. I am passing The Darkness House, Shivering House, Jaguar House, Razor House –

F: It's our ancient belief system, how the world came into being. Everything has spirit – the stones, the cacti, the animals, the fruit, the hummingbirds, the people, the earth – we're all one, coming from one, and returning to one.

To death. Being dead is our natural state. We are dead and then we become alive, and then we return to being dead.

SPEAKER: Let us take on the old Mayan ways and let the soul be dual: First 'Ch'ulel', the indestructible, eternal part; second, the companion protector, taking the form of a wild animal. Let us go back to our home, already inhabited by C'Ahau, lord of the stags. Let us shout from the mountaintops, howl like the coyote, scream like the mountain cat. Let us imitate the roar of the puma and the jaguar.

F: I am the Mayan goddess Xquic, the Blood Woman, she who has spilled and gathered much blood.

2: Once upon a time there was a beautiful teenager ripped apart in a horrific bus accident, who not only survived, but thrived.

4: Once upon a time there was a political activist, who went in the rain in her wheelchair to a demonstration only hours before she died.

3: Once upon a time there was an adulterous wife who had an affair with Trotsky, who was assassinated in her family home.

1: Once upon a time there was a dying painter who turned up to her last exhibition by ambulance, on her skeleton-festooned deathbed.

F: Am I not done yet?

Look at the cadaver dressed for day of the dead in her frippery and gaudy finery. Put red lipstick on the corpse. See the dead walk and grin. A conjuror's trick. Smoke and mirrors. Now you see me, now you see you me even more….

3: The long skirts, the jewels – diamond or paste, doesn't matter so long as they catch the light. The flowered, beribboned hair, perfumed and pomaded as surely as Marie Antoinette's.

F: But as a cadre, a peasant, one of the people. There's nothing privileged about me.

4: 'Dress is ideological, a class issue.'

1: Be careful! Don't be devoured by your frocks!

2: And the constant distraction of the burning cigarette in the hand, the dirty joke in the sailor's mouth, the filthy laugh, a promise in the eye.

They dance a sexy political march.

They hold the final image, fuck you smile, fists raised, out of which comes:

15.

Individual responses to her art no.4

(My Dress Hangs There.)

It's political. This native, traditional dress hangs against the Manhattan skyline, suspended on a ribbon between two pedestals: one has a toilet bowl and the other a golf trophy. It's all about crap – the worthless shit that's valued; this disposable, competitive culture that's just about sport. And there's Trinity Church, where a large painted S transforms the crucifix into a dollar sign, meanwhile the 99 per cent gather in breadlines and demonstrations, ignored and overlooked. It's brilliant, a condemnation of capitalism, but with humour. It bites, but it's almost funny. I never knew until I saw it you could paint from a Marxist perspective, and with wit.

16.

Title projected: MARXISM WILL HEAL THE SICK

1 is flanked by Man 1 and Man 2, police figures in sombre suits as in 'Self Portrait with Cropped Hair'.
At times they speak together in chorus, but later it becomes dialogue.

1: They came at night. The noise on the stairs and then the door bursting in. I wasn't allowed to dress, just a blanket thrown over my nightclothes. Shoes, no socks. No bag, wallet, nothing, just –

MAN 2: – Helping with enquiries.

1: So they pulled me in.

1& MAN 2: What we don't like

1: they told me,

1& MAN 2: is anarchists and rioters.

1: And I realised I was a suspect. And I realised I was the enemy.

The scene resembles an interrogation.

1: I am not a rioter.
I am not an anarchist.

(Beat.)

In fact, any group is in itself contradictory to the concept and definition of the term.

(Beat.)

The whole idea of anarchism is to be without structure, or organisation.

MAN 2: You seem to know an unhealthy amount about something you claim not to be involved with.

1: Knowing what a word means doesn't make you a supporter. Knowledge doesn't make you a suspect.

MAN 1: So why does your name keep coming up, and your face on surveillance photographs taken at demonstrations?

1: It's my democratic right to make peaceful protest.

MAN 1: Breaking and entering without permission. Disrupting official business. Interfering with government property and the running of daily office…

MAN 2: Doesn't sound very peaceful to me.

1: That's a matter of opinion.

MAN 2: No. That's a matter of law.

MAN 1: Preventing legally elected legislators from carrying out their work is neither peaceful, legal, nor is it democratic.

1: When that work doesn't follow agreed procedures, when it undermines personal liberties, to act becomes a duty.

MAN 2: Are you paranoid?

MAN 1: I don't see an advancing army. I don't see a dictator, do you?

1: It's the evolution of control. Once, it was through might. Now it's economics. Big money speaks and we are meant to follow, but when we say no
(Transition from interrogation dynamic to monologue.)
we discover a tougher skin.
(As opening of scene – addressing audience.)
Before, I'd thought that was what we were: vulnerable organisms at large in the world – just tiny creatures with their skeletons on the inside and the soft bits outside, unprotected. Timid, half asleep, concerned only with personal comfort. Cocooned – this waking slumber. And then suddenly the layers were torn off. I moved out into the new air, afraid, shivering – vulnerable – and saw there were others – others like me blinking, waking, rubbing their eyes – I was not alone… Together we discovered our purpose: no longer sleepwalking, but aware of our being, our individuality, our independence. The cataracts that had covered our eyes fell away. We stood up, together. It was 4 A.M. and we faced the new morning.

Title: FRIDA'S MANIFESTO ON ART AND POLITICS

An audio of Frida's manifesto on art and politics in Spanish and translation:

PF: 'Los creadores de belleza deben invertir sus mayores esfuerzos con el objetivo de materializar un arte valioso para el pueblo, y nuestro objetivo supremo en el arte, que es hoy una expresión para el placer individual, es crear belleza para todos, belleza que ilumina e incita a la lucha.'

TRANSLATOR: 'The makers of beauty must invest their greatest efforts in the aim of materialising an art valuable to the people, and our supreme objective in art, which is today an expression for individual pleasure, is to create beauty for all, beauty that enlightens and stirs to struggle.'

17.

Title projection: COMRADE FASHIONISTA

A figure appears live, as a model on the fashion show runway, and simultaneously mediatised, reporting backstage at a 'glamorous' photo-shoot, busy, chaotic, the 'Fridas/models' being made-up. In hyped-up Style magazine-speak:

MEDIATISED: With her fondness for role-play, striking poses and attitudes, no other cadre stylista has such a skilful theatrical rhetoric of the body in pain.
No other face pulls off archness better – that statement monobrow, the perfect foil for frilly things. Bedecked in costume, the archetypal pre-Columbian goddess meets panto trannie with that little moustache and each finger adorned with rings.
Possibly because she resembles a glamorous Long John Silver with her hand-tooled couture peg leg, she is an excellent vessel for kitsch. Bring on the frou-frou – long skirts, voluminous petticoats hand embroidered with smutty one-liners, the German braided topknot is Eva Braun meets Carmen Miranda – the Teutonic meets Tehuana – no wonder she graced the covers of French and American *Vogue.*
Bow down to the powers of Madam Wow and the style secrets of her little red book: *Comrade Fashionista.*

The same figure comments, live:

MODEL LIVE: I was the regional mascot, proof of belonging, of commitment, of a sound ideology. I was a breathing political statement, ideology embodied, culture personified.

F: No one can question your commitment to place, your national identity, when you're dressed like this.

MODEL LIVE: Look at me: for I represent my small, brave little country – its rich traditions and treasures, its history and heritage.

F: I thought I belonged, was significant, but I was little more than an exotic bloom my husband wore in his lapel.

MODEL LIVE: The gawdy bird, the flash of iridescence, dead at 47, forgotten by 48.

F: But I rise. Like the mythic bird the Resplendent Quetjal, I take flight, leaving opals on common stones as I pass.

The images from the fashion photo shoot become live camera filming several of the figures 'playing' with toys, which appear projected full size: A toy tram and bus. They collide and smash. Repeatedly.

As they do so:

18.

Individual responses to her art no. 5

(Self portrait in Tehuana headdress.)

I am all judder like the exposed nerves that extend, like taproots, like a psychic web from your head dress, from your staring crying face, crowned, as always, with your thoughts of him.

19.

In transition between scenes: A video of a toy tram and bus colliding and smashing, with snippets from the news on the radio:

VOICE C: *(V/O.)* …The handrail entered the body at abdomen level and exited via…

VOICE A: *(V/O.)* … a shattered pelvis from the impact of vehicles in the accident…

VOICE B: *(V/O.)*… breaking the spinal column in three places, dislocating her left limb and…

Transition into:

1: Shall we continue, tell it?

F: I'm so tired of telling, I'm forgetting how it all went.
Is that part of the process? The moving on, the letting go…?

2: First you dismember, then you remember…

F: So you want to tell from there, from my accident?

Projection: THE SURVIVOR OF A ROAD ACCIDENT

F: How do you make art out of pain – life from a body if not dead, then already rotting?
They said my body smelt like old meat left out in the sun and my heart was quivering on a butcher's slab with Diego's cleaver already in it.

2: Split.

F: There are two of me. Maybe more.
The dream of a girl before polio, before my two accidents, before the tram's hand-rail spliced me like an over-ripe fruit, impaled, spilling. I passed out, and came to minutes, days, moments later, and it was snowing gold filaments and I was naked and gold plated, covered in gilt dust from a painter's bag.

3: An angel!

4: The angel of death!

2: Goddess Xquic, the Blood Woman!

F: Dusted with gold, laid out on a billiard table – thrown out with the rubbish, left with the other damaged goods to die in the sun. And I realised the dying ballerina, the jointed, bleeding doll from the road accident was me – arranged on the green baize of a snooker table like a joint of meat on the plastic grass in the butcher's shop window.
But I would not submit to this

3: murder by life.

F: and dragged myself up, a Frankenstein with the black clumsy stitches,

4: a steel jacket

3: a corset

2: a string of hail marys

F: holding the mess of me together.

The abattoir of my body

1 transforms into a doctor with a white coat and puts F into a corset. Voice-over, slightly overlapping and fading in and out, as various radio/tv news announcers:

VOICE A: *(V/O.)* The collarbone was broken, as was the third and fourth ribs. Her spinal column was shattered…

VOICE B: *(V/O.)* The left leg had eleven fractures, the right foot dislocated and crushed. A deep abdominal wound…

VOICE C: *(V/O.)* The left shoulder was out of joint and the pelvis broken in three places in the lumbar region…

VOICE B: *(V/O.)* The handrail entered the body on the left side at abdomen level….

Radio fades out.

3: But these are the easy damages, made of flesh and bone. They don't include the deeper hurts. The terminated dreams, the broken futures, the severed plans. It omits the sleepless nights and the fears at that small hour when she would lie on her back in her bed and stare up at herself in the mirror suspended by her mother from the canopy. It was almost a relief when she finally picked up the brushes and began to paint.

F: I lived, dying.

1 *(As Dr.)*: *(Reading from a letter.)* 'A little while ago… I was a little girl who walked through a world of colours, of hard and tangible forms. Everything was mysterious and concealed something. I took pleasure in deciphering, in

learning, as in a game. If only you knew how terrible it is suddenly to know everything… as if a flash of lightning lit up the earth. Now I live on a dolorous planet, transparent like ice…'

Continuous action into:

20.

A psychology test – F with Doctor.

1/Dr: 'Hate

F: Cannibal flower.

1/Dr: Pain

F: Flame. Rises and devours.

1/Dr: Love.

F: Grows in red, broken, anguished lines.

1/Dr: Mirth.

F: Tissue of life, with cells and suns.

1/Dr: Pain

F: Deep-purple wheel, jagged edged saw.'

Change.

Pain.
I want to speak of pain.
I know the body prepped, sedated and strapped to the operating table, the section uncovered where seconds later the surgeon will make his incision. His incision, for it is always a man. It is women who feed and dress me, play with my dolls, plait my hair. It is men who prep sedate and strap me to the operating table.
Thirty-four times.
I went through this thirty-four times.
Tree of hope, hold firm.

Image of Tree of Hope: Two Fridas. One is lying down on a hospital bed after a recent operation, the sheet revealing her bloodied back, the other one sits beside, in full Oaxaca dress, holding a back brace and a message saying 'Tree of Hope, Remain Strong'.

2: Take care:
Complain too much and they'll put you to sleep.
Challenge their treatment of your damaged dragging form and they'll zip you up in a concrete suit, a corset of steel, s-t-r-e-t-c–h-e-d, suspended, hung from your chin until the plaster dries, then cast into bed for a year.
'Lie down. Stay still. Can't you just lie there, quiet, and let those bones knit?'
At night I can hear the fibres meshing:

OTHERS: Knit one, purl one, slip one, knit one, pass slipped stitch over (x3.)

F: Let me 'proceed urgently to surrendering myself to the arms of morpheus for a few hours, as prescribed by herr doktor.'

2: Oh I'm feeling so fine, doctor, thank you. I'm mending, I'm darned, cross-stitched, cabled together.
Don't put the hollow steel reed in my vein, its sleepy tranquilising balm freezing my blood. Don't dip the opiate into my vein. Demerol. Morphine. I'll get a habit, herr doktor. You know I'll love it.

21.

Individual responses to her art no. 6

(Itzcuintli dog and me.)

4: In photographs, she's stoned. And in the paintings she always has a cigarette in her hand, or a joint in one of those metal pincer roach holders pimps in American 1970s movies use, so they won't stain their fingers.
In self-portraits the nicotine's always there.
I was at an exhibition and a curator, also a smoker, explained the Italian technique sfumato, which she used for the background. A swirly ashy grey, like the tiny dog with the zinc-coloured skin, matching the burnished

metal of her dress.
'Sfumato: smoked,' he said. It was the only time she used the technique in a portrait, her legs crossed, joint in hand, ash and silver grey and smoke. 'The patron saint of smokers,' he said.
'The Madonna of Marijuana.'

22.

Ensemble involved in creating a dressing of still lives for painting. Fruit, flowers, marigolds. 3 writes in a journal.

3: 'Auxochrome – chromophore.
She who wears the colour.
He who sees the colour.
… After all the hours lived through ...
There is cellular arrangement. There is movement.
There is light. All centres are the same…
Auxochrome – chromophore.
It was the thirst of many years restrained in our body….
My blood is the miracle which runs in the vessels of the air from my heart to yours…'

F: At last – an exhibition in my own country. I went in the ambulance, and was carried at my husband's insistence on a stretcher into the gallery – and there was my bed from home, festooned with day of the dead skeletons and photographs, my personal tat.
And then I realised it was an art installation and it was me who was going to be installed.
The artist's last act: Dying as art.
Good business, great publicity.
My husband the communist –
such a gifted capitalist.

She is installed in her exhibition bed.
The dressings of still lives adorn it.

When I was encased in plaster – like a coffin – when I was buried alive, bound to my bed – all those hours spent looking up into the mirror, preparing poses, practising expressions, perfecting the mask – it was a relief to have my father's brushes finally pushed by my mother into my hands. I became the doctor I wanted to be before the accident, and did surgery on myself, removing my skin and flesh, displaying the heart, the foetus, the spine – and all anatomically precise. A pastime, she called it.

3: No longer a narcissus, in love with his own reflection, but an artist, a creator, making some thing.

F: Though I couldn't make a child, what I desired.

3: Not being a mother makes you the eternal adolescent – always hovering on the threshold but never graduating to adulthood. You're always the child, the off-spring, the daughter. Never fully grown up. Never given the responsibility for the life of others – not just protecting life, but creating it – conceiving, conceptualising…

F: You should try painting.

3: Like you? Bleeding, weeping, bristling with 67 nails and 9 arrows; naked, broken, cracked open, plants consuming you, half buried in a desert, your face on a wounded deer, a choker of thorns around your neck, an open third eye, your head emerging from your dead mother's sex, the weeping delorosa watching on.

F: I paint my reality.

3: They called you a surrealist.

2&4: 'The pretty ribbon tied around the bomb.'

F: My husband may have been a muralist on a massive scale, but my work was truly epic – a monsterist – and all on 12 by 15 inches. The precision learnt in my father's photographic studio – sure hands, a miniaturist's eye for detail.
But we are too sombre! Dying, like art, is a serious business, so we need tequila!
I drank to drown my sorrows.
But the damn things learnt to swim.
Music!

They dance tango.

23.

Choral. A re-set.

1: Shall we continue, tell it?

F: I'm tired of telling.
I want to smoke. Keep death on the lips.

1: Let's go on.

F: I'm tired. I don't remember. I don't want to remember.
I ache. Sometimes I can't get out of bed for the pain.

4: So you have everyone else run around after you…

F: Pain in my bones. I can feel them rubbing together, chaffing, like a splintered chicken bone. And then there's the scar tissue – those nubs of flesh, the ridges from where the skin didn't heal, or forgot to, or couldn't be bothered to, or wasn't allowed to.
'Open her up again, doctor!'
Eight operations in one year.

3: It doesn't take long to learn that special attention comes with illness and surgery and being the patient.

2: Pity is stronger than love.

4: You can't leave an invalid, you can't leave a martyr. You can't leave a saint.

3: 'The poor thing.'

2: 'But isn't she marvelous, considering?'

3: 'So brave! So uncomplaining!'

F: I am not sick. I am broken, there's a difference.
Why do you torment me?

1: It's all part of the process.

2: The moving on.

4: The taking leave.

2: The dying.

F: Am I not done yet?

WE SEE THE STARS.

SPEAKER: I am in the realm of Xibalbá, the K'iche Shades, the dark rift in the Milky Way. The lords of this realm emaciate people, waste them away. Ahaltocob, Stabbing Demon, catches people and pierces them til they die. Xic and Patan cause sudden death on the road.

F: Is that why I'm here? Are the lords of the underworld angry with me? I gave so many blood offerings, but escaped sudden death on the road: Xic and Patan, who caused the streetcar to collide with the bus, who brought about my major accident.

3: Sssssh, chamaca Friduchita… Let the bones heal.

1: It's a delirium brought on by the morphine.

F: Am I hallucinating? But it all feels so real.

4: You're dreaming.

3: Dreamy dreamy dream.

2: You're dead, dreaming of life.

F: Alive, dreaming of death.

2: He dances, le pelona, the bald one, around the bed at night.

3: And so she stares upwards into the mirror hung by her parents from the canopy, stares upwards into the familiar face –

1: the unblinking eye, the monobrow

3: – stares, and paints.

1: Once upon a time there was an opium addict who drank one bottle of tequila every day.

2: Once upon a time there was a spinal injuries patient who transformed her agonies into paintings going at $5.4 million a time.

4: Once upon a time there was a woman who defied conventions and made her own rules.

3: Once upon a time there was an icon, who gave birth to herself.

F: And such a life. Three children lost, and so much more.

24.

Individual responses to her art no.7

(The Two Fridas.)

1: The heart is a hollow muscle, a pump with four chambers and four valves, with an internal wall of tissue, the septum, dividing left and right.
An average heart beats 72 times per minute, that's 2.5 billion times over the course of an average 65 years. It weighs ten ounces, or 275 grams in the average woman.
So why does it hurt?
How can an organic mechanised pump responsible for the circulatory system cause such pain?
They said it was a bigger than average heart and she was far from being an average woman, so it didn't fit, and ached, constrained by its bone cage.
So she flipped it out, let it rest on her left breast like a big red rose against the white lace high necked blouse, a pulsing rosette against the cobalt blue peasant shirt: best in show.

We see the two Fridas

Into:

25.

Projection: FRIDA'S FIESTAS: RITUAL TO CONSECRATE A TALISMAN TO SANTA MUERTE, THE WHITE LADY OF MEXICO

Mediatised. Cooking Frida (F2.) appears with another, different kind of recipe:

F2: Take one statue of Santa Muerte, and if that isn't available, a prayer card or an image of her will do; some red ribbon or cord; a glass of fresh, clean water; one white candle of substantial size – this consecration ceremony takes place over three nights, so be sure you have a candle big enough – and a pendant – ideally

Santa Muerte, but you can substitute a skull, skeleton, or grim reaper instead.

F: Painting – my salvation, the thing that gave meaning to this interlude called life. Everything else failed me.

F2: Cleanse the pendant and chain by rubbing with a little alcohol. Then put aside and allow it to dry. If you are using a prayer card or paper image of Santa Muerte, place it under the candleholder on your altar. Place the glass of water near the candle. Water is the basic offering to the spirit. You may also offer bread, fruit, or other small offering in a bowl, but what she really likes is a lit cigarette, or joint.

F: Bees buzz in the key of A. But only when they're rested. When they tire, the buzz changes key…
I'm changing key. I'm nearly done.

F2: On a Tuesday or Thursday night during a Full Moon, light the candle and pray to Santa Muerte, asking for her protection. Really speak from your heart, make a connection with the spirit.

F: The average human gets through 900 skins in a lifetime. What number are you on?

F2: When you have finished your prayer, fold the pendant and cord in a handkerchief and place it in front of Santa Muerte, allowing the candle to burn down one third.

F: I'm shedding the final skin.

F2: Then, snuff out the candle and take the handkerchief and place it in the bottom of a drawer.

F: I'm almost done with looking.

F2: Repeat this procedure on the second and third nights, allowing the candle to burn down completely. The pendant is then ready to serve.

F: What use is it to see when the hand is no longer steady? I can't paint for pain, and pain relief brings tremors. This blurring. The colours are muddy, paint caked on. My hands shake – devastating little earthquakes.

3: And so she stares upwards into the mirror hung by her parents above her bed,

1: the unblinking eye

3: stares

4: but no longer paints.

Choral:

1: We know things, we women who do not sleep…. *(repeated.)*

2: we who pretend

4: who have doubts

3: who register. We the cheated women

1: the broken

2: defiant

3: listeners and watchers

1: we know things

2: we women who speak the sweating small hour horrors

3: as the spider crawls across the chest

4: and into the lurching cavity of the heart.

2: We survivors.

4: We mourners.

1: We celebrants.

WE SEE THE STARS.

WE SEE THE SPEAKER, WHO WATCHES BUT DOES NOT SPEAK.

(Rosaries/rituals.)

2: Blessed Saint Frida of spondylitis, curvature of the spine, name saint of the peg legs, the polios, the corset-wearing spina bifidas

3: Patron saint of the childless, the infertile, the fractured pelvis which won't hold life to full term.

F: Pull down the shutters.

2: Crybaby of Coyocan, martyr Frida delorosa, the virgin lacrimorum.

F: Close these eyes.

1: La Huesuda, Lady of bones, she who is shattered and pieced together again.

3: Mayauel, goddess of all intoxicants, eater of sins.

F: I'm done.

2: Patron of love, beauty, flowers, and prostitutes.

F: I have passed through the 9 hells, K'iche shades, the dark rift visible in the Milky Way.

4: Our Lady of the Dead. She who protects, inspires, who exists in eternal darkness.

1: She who is four faces of the moon.

F: I have shed my skins.
Let me go, return to where I have always been.
A place of the living, a place of the dead.
Let me return to the dark: forgetfulness.

ALL: La Santa Meurte, goddess of death.

F: Let the going be joyful.
And may I never come back.

End.

cosy

Kaite O'Reilly in association with Wales Millennium Centre and The Llanarth Group, supported by Unlimited.

Cosy premiered at Wales Millennium Centre on 8 March 2016

Cast

ROSE	Sharon Morgan
ED	Ri Richards
CAMILLE	Ruth Lloyd
GLORIA	Llinos Daniel
ISABELLA	Bethan Rose Young
MAUREEN	Sara Beer

Directed by	Phillip Zarrilli
Designed by	Simon Banham
Lighting by	Ace McCarron
Costume by	Holly McCarthy
Associate Producer	Sandra Bendelow
Assistant Producer	Tom Wentworth

Characters

ROSE
76. Mother to three daughters:

ED
55.

CAMILLE
50.

GLORIA
48.

ISABELLA
16. Camille's daughter.

MAUREEN
Rose's companion.

A large sitting room in a once grand house.

What follows is the rehearsal draft.
Some changes may be made in production.

PRESET

An empty space in pre-dawn light – settled shadows, indiscernible shapes. ROSE's voice, intimate.

ROSE V/O: That muffled silence at 3 A.M. – feeling the pump pump pump of your heart and the jaw going, any nonsense, any rubbish, anything just not to let the silence in, not let the pause fill. Those quiet hours of the night when you're there, waiting for dawn. Waiting for the first trace of light, scanning the sky, holding your breath almost, willing the light, yes, willing the light –

Time passes, the lights change, revealing:

ONE

A large sitting room. Once gracious, it is now neglected and filled with wing chairs covered in dustsheets. CAMILLE stands with her suitcase. ED looks at her, waiting.

ED: Put the case down.

(CAMILLE doesn't.)

Sit.

(CAMILLE doesn't.)

That's right.

(CAMILLE stands and looks.)

Still the old homestead. Hasn't changed.

CAMILLE: I thought you might have modernised it a bit. You know, pulled up the lino, sandblasted the floorboards. There's some lovely original tiles hidden under the runner in the entrance hall – blue, ochre and – sorry, I couldn't help noticing when I came in.

ED: You never did, before.

CAMILLE: Professional eye?

ED: And all that.

CAMILLE: You could add a cornice to this room. Clean up that central rose – all the detail's been blurred by layers of slapped on gloss, can you see? It'd put value on the house.

ED: Would it?

CAMILLE: It's the little things. Like – that wall, for example...

ED: Yeah.

CAMILLE: Put back in the old fireplace and – no... Open it up, just open it up, expose the square and fill it with stuffed animals – taxidermy is so 20th century retro – whitewash the brickwork and...!! You can do wonders simply with a hole in the wall nowadays.

ED: Really?

CAMILLE: When it's done well. A room like this is a blank canvas. The artistry you could make... with the right artist, of course. No use going for a Jackson Pollock when what you need is a Cezanne.

ED: We like it how it is.

CAMILLE: But if you opened your imagination to the possibilities... I'm saying this to my clients all the time. It's a fundamental human trait, resistance to change. But that's the one certainty we have in this life, in fact the only certainty: Change. So don't resist the inevitable, that's what I say.

ED: It suits us.

CAMILLE: I daresay sleeping in caves suited the Neanderthals, but in order to progress, you have to have imagination and vision.

ED: It does us.

CAMILLE: Like daubing blood on the walls probably 'did' for the early homo sapiens. You don't want to be living in the dark ages, with blood decorating your walls, do you?

ED: No.

CAMILLE: Well then. A little ironic rag-rolling could work wonders on this place.

ED: Tea?

CAMILLE: Or just whack it out. Get rid of the dark wood and belt it all out with white – no, taupe, a semolina sort of colour… Bare boards, a coarse homespun rag rug, maybe some simple Shaker furniture and Navaho-inspired touches. Moroccan influence is so yesterday. Appalachian Spring – that's the stuff. You belt it all out in *nougat*, put in some up-cycled furniture, dried prairie grass and strategically placed wooden clogs and you'd make a fortune. It wouldn't last ten minutes on an estate agent's books.

ED: It isn't for sale.

CAMILLE: But think of the profit you could make!

ED: And where would we live?

CAMILLE: With the profits you could make from this place, you could buy somewhere else and live very comfortably. Very comfortably indeed. Somewhere more suited to your lifestyle and aspirations. More compact.

ED: Bijou?

CAMILLE: Just think of the time you'd save on cleaning. A nice little bungalow or apartment. No more aching limbs dragging the old vacuum cleaner about the place. I know what it's like.

ED: Up the stairs.

CAMILLE: Exactly. And how many flights do you have? I think you can see my point.

ED: Will you have a coffee?

CAMILLE: Water. Bottled, if you have it. I like it straight from the source.

ED leaves, CAMILLE continues, raising her voice so she can still be heard.

But it's up to you, of course. I'm only thinking of you. It's not often I give out my advice for free – in fact, some pay a very high price for my thoughts and I don't think I'd be boasting to say a very high price indeed. But they get what they're paying for. Value. Value for money, that's me.

She goes to sit on a chair – inspects it and dusts it with her scarf. A woman, MAUREEN, enters unnoticed by CAMILLE. She is wearing a mint green hospital gown under a man's suit jacket and steel-capped boots. She propels what seems to be a blood-filled catheter on wheels. CAMILLE spreads a scarf over one of the chairs and is about to sit, when:

MAUREEN: That's my mother's chair.

CAMILLE: Is it?

MAUREEN: Yes.

CAMILLE pauses, looks MAUREEN over, then moves to another chair.

And that one is.

In fact, all of them are. My mother's chairs. In the plural.

CAMILLE: There's quite a few of them.

MAUREEN: Well she liked sitting down. In fact, I can't remember her doing anything else. Some might have memories of their mothers knitting or baking or standing, washing up at the sink. Mine just sat. There's no need to be nervous.

CAMILLE: I'm not.

MAUREEN: It's just furniture. My mother's furniture. There's nothing to worry about.

CAMILLE: I'm not. The chairs… . They're probably antique. They've certainly been around longer than I have.

MAUREEN: Just shabby old sticks of furniture.

CAMILLE: Heirlooms.

MAUREEN: Tat.

CAMILLE: Mementoes.

MAUREEN: Shite.

Well, have a look at them: there's no style to them, no class at all. But what else can you expect? You can take a child out of the gutter, but you'll never take the gutter out of the child and I think this choice of chairs proves that. They speak for themselves and there's a lot of profanities. She picked them. And we have to live with them. And doesn't it bloody show.

(Beat.)

I'm a walking miracle me.

CAMILLE: Are you?

MAUREEN: I pass blood.

CAMILLE: Do you?

MAUREEN: Have the medical profession in a spin. A wonder. A legend in my own diagnosis. I'm a passing-blooder.

CAMILLE: So you said.

MAUREEN: Look at me here with my bucket of blood.

(They look.)

I'm on my way to the garden. It's what they recommend.

CAMILLE: Fresh air and exercise?

MAUREEN: No – for the roses. They flourish on it. All the books and television programmes say so.

CAMILLE: Oh.

MAUREEN: You have to be careful with manure – people think it's safe, but oh no. Diseased. Fatal for children's eyes.

CAMILLE: Well, you should have no trouble with the blood, then.

MAUREEN: None at all.

She leaves.

ED enters, with a glass of whiskey

ED: We didn't have any bottled water, so I brought this instead.

CAMILLE: It's a little early in the day for spirits, thank you.

ED: Who asked you?

(ED drinks her whisky. Silence.)

This is nice.

CAMILLE: Yes.

ED: Having conversation.
Exchanging views and opinions.
Shooting the breeze.

CAMILLE: Yes.

ED: You never said what you were here for.

CAMILLE: No, I didn't.

A long not altogether comfortable pause

ED: Perhaps it's serendipity?

CAMILLE: Serendipity?

(Silence.)

Is there anything you want to tell me?

ED: Is there anything you want to tell me?

(Silence.)

I'll pop your case upstairs to your room, if you like.

CAMILLE: I would like. Thank you.

ED exits with bag, meeting ISABELLA entering with a mobile phone. ED points.

ED: In there.

ISABELLA enters, putting away her phone.

CAMILLE: So… .?

ISABELLA: She's on her way.

CAMILLE: You're sure?

ISABELLA: So she said.

CAMILLE: And since when have we been able to trust a single thing that girl says? What did you tell her?

ISABELLA: I said there was a crisis and we all needed to be on hand.

CAMILLE: A crisis?

ISABELLA: Yes.

CAMILLE: You actually said a *crisis*?

ISABELLA: Yes. What else would you call it?

CAMILLE: A *situation*. What we have is a *situation*. You go saying things like 'crisis' to her and it'll be full scale operatics – screaming and fainting and the beating of breasts and blaming. Yes, *blaming*. Nobody does passing the buck quite as well as she does. Some might call it an accomplishment.

ISABELLA: So why did you ask me to call her?

CAMILLE: What?

ISABELLA: Why did you ask me to call her if you don't like her?

CAMILLE: I didn't say I didn't like her! How could you say that? What possibly would give you the impression I don't like my little sister?

ISABELLA: Inference.

CAMILLE: Excuse me?

ISABELLA: I *inferred* it. From your tone.

CAMILLE: My tone.

ISABELLA: And the fact you haven't seen her for years and you don't seem to want her here.

CAMILLE: Of course I want her here! She's family and it's a family crisis, so of course by definition I want the family here! That's why I asked you to call her in the first place. Honestly!

ISABELLA: Can't see why you couldn't have called her yourself.

CAMILLE: Because we're not speaking, you know that. And don't talk to me about tone, Miss Holier Than Thou tone. I'll give you tone, Miss Christ Himself Wouldn't Have Been So Fair tone.

ISABELLA: I'm sorry.

CAMILLE: Yes, well. I'll have you know I'm very sensitive to tones. In fact, I'm known for it, famed for my sensitivity. I'm like a bat or a dog, hear registers that other human ears wouldn't even imagine! Couldn't even conceive! Something to do with the follicles in the inner ear. And let me tell you something else, Ms Butter Wouldn't Melt: Being judgemental is very oppressive. Very oppressive indeed.

ISABELLA: I'm sorry.

(Beat.)

I'm sure they won't send out bailiffs.

CAMILLE: Don't even say that word!

ISABELLA: I bet it's not as bad as you think.

CAMILLE: So rather than be proved wrong, I'd prefer to sit it out here for a night or two.

ISABELLA: Our personal development tutor at school says we should confront our problems, not run away from them.

CAMILLE: I am not running away. I'm hiding. Just – stay the age you are now.

ISABELLA: I don't think that's physiologically possible. Or desirable, really. I like growing older.

CAMILLE: Let's see how you feel when the pop-up ads every time you go on-line are for funeral expenses and Tena Lady. It used to be sparkly dresses and inappropriate footwear… We'll see if you still like growing older when you're by-passed for a ten-year-old 'who better epitomises the youthful vibe the company wants to project.' And whilst we're on the subject, you need to eat more liver.

ISABELLA: – ?

CAMILLE: You're anaemic. You're washed out looking, a sort of nondescript beige. Aren't you feeling well?

ISABELLA: I'm fine.

CAMILLE: Have you a temperature?

ISABELLA: I'm fine.

CAMILLE: Oh, pay no attention to your silly Mamu. She's just tense and stupid and hands up, admit it – hormonal. So she's sorry. I'm sorry. Do you forgive me?

ISABELLA: Yes.

CAMILLE: Good. Miss silky face. Miss unlined, plumped, taut collagen face. Miss I remember when I had skin like that face.
(Tenderly.) You know something?

ISABELLA: What?

CAMILLE: A little bit of blusher wouldn't hurt. Or what's that newer one? Mineral bronzer. Yes, just a tad, just the slightest, lightest sprinkling… Hopeless for anyone over thirty-five, like brick dust in cracks, so use it while you can.
I know: How about we make a day of it when this is all over? You and me, down in the big smoke, getting a make-over. Wouldn't that be fun? Shall we get ourselves made over?

ISABELLA: I'm fine how I am.

CAMILLE: Well that's a matter of opinion.

ISABELLA: I like how I am.

CAMILLE: Wan?
Ashen?
Drab?

ISABELLA: Yes.
Anyway, it suits me.

CAMILLE: Says who?

ISABELLA: Me.

CAMILLE: That doesn't count.

ISABELLA: Okay, people, people say.

CAMILLE: Who? Which people?

ISABELLA: People. Just…

CAMILLE: Yes?

ISABELLA: People.

CAMILLE: Yes?

ISABELLA: Dan.

CAMILLE: Dan?

ISABELLA: Dan. Dan says it suits me.

CAMILLE: To look like the walking dead?

ISABELLA: Natural. He says he likes me looking natural.

CAMILLE: There's no such thing.

ISABELLA: He says he likes me without make-up, then.

CAMILLE: Oh. *(Realising.)* Oh… So are you and Dan… an item?

ISABELLA: An item?

CAMILLE: Yes… an *item*…

ISABELLA: What, like a tin of baked beans is an item?

CAMILLE: Are you seeing each other?

ISABELLA: Well, neither of us has a visual impairment, so –

CAMILLE: – Are you going out?

ISABELLA: We're not agoraphobic.

CAMILLE: Are you dating?

ISABELLA: *'Dating'?!*

CAMILLE: Okay: Is he inserting his penis into your vagina on a regular basis?

ISABELLA: What!!?

CAMILLE: Well, the euphemisms weren't working, so thought I'd cut straight to the chase… .

ISABELLA: I can't believe you just said that.

CAMILLE: Well, you're an adult, so I should start treating you more as an adult, so –

ISABELLA: I'm sixteen.

CAMILLE: Exactly, an adult, so –

ISABELLA: All I said is he doesn't like it when I wear make-up and then you get all creepy porno on me.

CAMILLE: Let me tell you something, woman to woman: May I? Men always say that. They always say you're beautiful and you don't need make-up.

ISABELLA: There you are, then.

CAMILLE: They say that because they think it'll get them laid.

ISABELLA: Not all of them.

CAMILLE: Most. But others say that to give you self-esteem, to make you feel so good about yourself that you'll show a little pride in your appearance and head straight to the nearest beauty counter and get the full slap. They're only trying to hide their base superficiality when they say 'natural'. It's synthetic and latex and thigh-high rubber boots all the way with men. Trust me. What they really want is you primped and plumped, ready for the sack.

ISABELLA: Dan doesn't.

CAMILLE: Yes, well, Dan's probably the exception.

ISABELLA: Yes.

CAMILLE: Dan's embraced his inner female so much he's at risk of becoming a lesbian.

ISABELLA: He is not!

CAMILLE: He's been sexually modified –

ISABELLA: Stop it!

CAMILLE: – gender-fluid from having a virago for a mother.

ISABELLA: He's a feminist and he likes women and

CAMILLE: Oh God, that bathroom full of mooncups and lunar calendars and offerings to Demeter, goddess of the hearth…

ISABELLA: I really don't want to talk about this with you.

CAMILLE: Oh, come on! Don't get uptight. I reared you to be free from sexual hang-ups and frustration and thinking you have to wear mascara or shave under your arms… I raised you to feel you had CHOICE. The anti-grooming thing was reverse psychology, by the way.

ISABELLA: I shave.

CAMILLE: Your face, by the feel of it. That's from an imbalance in hormones: too much testosterone from not enough sex and having to be the man in the relationship.

ISABELLA: Don't speak about my relationship when you don't know the first thing about it!

CAMILLE: So it *is* a relationship, then!

ISABELLA: God!

CAMILLE: And you're frustrated, I can tell, I know that look, that feeling… It's terrible, isn't it, when you start getting all sexed-up

ISABELLA: Mam!

CAMILLE: just craving for it all the time – any hour, any place – like animals rutting and snuffling and sucking and licking – I know, really – I recognise a frustrated woman when I see one.

ISABELLA: I'm not! And that's none of your business, anyway.

CAMILLE: Thought so.

ISABELLA: I'm not!

(She exits.)

CAMILLE: Thank you, God, she's still a virgin.

ROSE: And will probably remain so until her late thirties after the trauma of that little exchange.

ROSE becomes apparent, in a wing chair reminiscent of rest homes that had been obscuring her from view.

CAMILLE: Don't do that! Are you alone, or are there more of your new *chums* hidden away in those death chairs? They're terrible! Like something out of God's Waiting room – a place to rest before assuming room temperature.

ROSE: Don't try to change the subject…

CAMILLE: You shouldn't have been listening. How long have you been there?

ROSE: All of your life, darling.

CAMILLE: I hate it when you look at me like that.

(Beat.)

I'm doing her a favour! It would be reprehensible if I let her loose on to the streets so soft – unformed. She's like those terrifying mice they breed in vivisection labs with all the inner organs on the outside – no backbone, no protection, no –

ROSE: – I never spoke to you like that.

CAMILLE: No. You didn't. And look at me.

(ROSE looks appraisingly. Pause.)

Have you ever thought about venetian blinds?

ROSE: Philosophically?

CAMILLE: As an alternative to the nets. I'm talking polished wooden lattice here, not the white plastic dentist's surgery variety. They're very Bali-esque.

ROSE: Don't you mean Balinese?

CAMILLE: No, that's a different vibe entirely… But then again, with the height of the ceiling, you could probably get away with swags…

Yeah… Not something I would usually recommend, it's passé and a little vulgar, but you know… you might just get away with it in this room…

ROSE: I'm rather fond of how it is, now.

CAMILLE: That's a joke, right?

ROSE: I couldn't imagine it any other way.

CAMILLE: Try.

ROSE: It'll see me out.

CAMILLE: You'll live to be ninety.

ROSE: Dear God, no. I don't want to be one of those breathing fossils from an earlier epoch lingering on, joints creaking, uterus sagging, everything giving out.
You're looking well.

CAMILLE: Really?

ROSE: Flushed. Vital.

CAMILLE: I feel like I've disappeared. I walk down the road in full sunlight, but I throw no shadow.

ROSE: That's what growing older does for you.

CAMILLE: When you're female. I don't see the silverback or old bull elephant at work being undermined just because their skin has lost some of its elasticity.

ROSE: What an exciting environment you work in.

CAMILLE: The older and wiser I get, the less substantial my opinion becomes. I'm invisible.

ROSE: With that high colour darling? Never.

CAMILLE: And on the street...? People walk into me, bash shoulders, heavy bags smacking into me as they hurry past.

ROSE: People hurry so much these days. And have you noticed they're always satchels? Big huge leather bags, reeking of pigs–

CAMILLE: – and they wallop them into my ribs, them hurrying on, as if they didn't see me.

ROSE: You reach a certain age and it happens.

CAMILLE: Like I'd evaporated. Gone in the sun.

ROSE: When I was younger, I was furious when builders on sites called out to me. I was enraged if they shouted or whistled, clinging like some Tarzan, some fellamelad to the roof of a house, sunning themselves on the tiles – full of themselves, proud of their little cocks, curled like hairless baby mammals in the nest of their crotches, singing, radio blaring… Have you noticed so many builders and hod-carriers seem to be deliriously happy and bursting with life? I hated it. It felt like an attack, an intrusion. What I'd give for that attention, now.

(Beat.)

It was supposed to be enough: having a husband, family, making a home, keeping house. Everything nice, tidy, in its place.

CAMILLE: Mam.

ROSE: And at the time I thought am I greedy, unwomanly – ungrateful – to want more? It's enough for other women, isn't it? And now, looking back… well, what I've done seems rather meagre.

CAMILLE: The alternative isn't any better. You give work everything and you're still only ever three pay cheques from the street.

ROSE: We never really talked about it, your father and I. Before we had a chance, you'd all arrived and he got ill. And we all know the rest.

CAMILLE: But that wouldn't have stopped you –

ROSE: – I had troubles, I had you; I had things to be getting on with –

CAMILLE: But there's always a solution or a remedy – you just all come together and –

ROSE: – What fantasy are you spinning, darling? We can't even all be in the same room together, never mind problem solve!

CAMILLE: But –

ROSE: – Some things, once they're broken, they can't be fixed.

ISABELLA: *(Entering, engrossed with ED.)* So it's all called *Maya* – illusion – or at least, that's what the Hindus call it, but there's a similar idea in Buddhism that you shouldn't get *attached* to anything, as it'll only make you miserable and it's a total waste of time, as everything's all just a figment of your imagination, anyway.

ROSE: *(Seeing ED enter with tea tray.)* Oh, good! Tea!

ED hands out cups, ISABELLA shadows her around the room.

ISABELLA: And then when you look at it from a scientific point of view, Time itself may just be an illusion dreamt up by the human brain. Can you believe that?! Mad, isn't it? So that feeling of time passing? It could be nothing more than the brain shifting and shunting – that's a technical term – *shunting* sensory information into the holding chamber of the memory. Amazing, isn't it!

ED: I only said it feels like an awful long time since I last saw you.

ISABELLA: *(Both exiting.)* It may be – or it may not! It's like I said, Time's weird. I mean, even Aristophanes complained about the moon's awkward twenty-nine and a half day cycle, and that was millennia ago…

They have gone. ROSE looks at CAMILLE.

ROSE: I warned you about choosing Mensa sperm. At least if you'd had a fling you might have known what you'd end up with.

MAUREEN enters, her catheter now empty.

CAMILLE: A superficial toe rag led by his dick and god knows from what sewer of a gene pool. No, my way was better: an envelope full of cash and a special delivery couriered over. A lovely hot, relaxing bath and dexterity with the turkey baster… No animals were harmed in the making of that child.

ROSE: But it must be disconcerting being out-classed intellectually by your teenaged daughter…?

MAUREEN: So cut her down to size a bit.

CAMILLE: I'm sorry, and you are…?

MAUREEN speaks as she crosses to the opposite exit. ROSE doesn't respond.

MAUREEN: Tall flowers get picked, or blown over by the wind, or trampled on by dogs.

CAMILLE: Excuse me?

MAUREEN: Show her who's boss. Don't let her get too big for her boots. She'll thank you for it, later.

CAMILLE: Really.

MAUREEN: When she discovers what a cesspit this is.

CAMILLE: Oh?

MAUREEN: What a nasty, unfair, bigoted, hierarchical, misogynistic, violent, patriarchal scum afloat a rock spinning in the empty universe she will. But don't mind me. What do I know?

She continues towards the exit. ROSE is being 'Mother'.

ROSE: Do you still take sugar, or is that too plebeian and so last season?

CAMILLE: I've never taken sugar. I'm allergic to sugar.

ROSE: Unfortunately, whatever doesn't kill us apparently makes us stronger. So I'll add two spoons, then.

End of scene.

TWO

ED, CAMILLE and ISABELLA are cleaning the room, removing the dustsheets and thinning out the numerous wing chairs.

CAMILLE: And it's such a lovely little restaurant – locally sourced organic meat, and vegetables from the allotments across the way. Ploughing the profit back into the community. I call that brilliant. Linked-up thinking. So village-minded for a city. And to think I only noticed it because we had difficulty finding a parking space. I'm amazed you haven't been.

ED: I don't get out much.

CAMILLE: And very happy to deliver, which is just as well considering the state of the kitchen. Talk about minimalist; everything's packed away.

ED: That's the way she likes it.

CAMILLE: And the cupboard was virtually bare.

ED: We weren't expecting company.

CAMILLE: So I ordered a mixed roast meat dinner for six, with an additional vegetarian option for one, just to be on the safe side. So that's us three, Mother, that strange little sidekick, you-know-who, and her plus one, she's bound to bring *someone.* All we need do now is to make a semblance of order in here.

ED: I wonder who she'll turn up with, this time?

CAMILLE: *(To ISABELLA.)* We've had everything from hermaphrodites to Amazonian pygmies, if memory serves me right. Your aunt's not the most conventional or stable of people. But credit where it's due, when it comes to 'significant others' she has a phenomenally broad repertoire. 'Fussy' isn't a word that springs to mind.

ED: She's been married so many times the only thing new to her was the cake.

CAMILLE: There's been a traditional white Church wedding, a humanist joining…

ED: A Druidic blessing on Anglesey.

CAMILLE: That New Age commitment ceremony on the beach in Cornwall with our feet in the tide.

ED: We all ended up in A&E.

ISABELLA: Why?

ED: Jellyfish stings.

CAMILLE: The tide was infested.

ED: Portugese Man o' War.

CAMILLE: Apparently some freak tide brought a colony of them from off the west coast of Australia. Wooshed them half way across the globe to Porthcurnick beach of all places, and right on the dot of the one hour chosen by our little sister out of the many thousand possible other hours to publically proclaim her devotion to a didgeridoo player from Hull. Imagine! They'd never seen anything like it before in Truro. They don't really go in for indigenous Antipodean wind instruments that side of Totnes. And the stings!

ED: Thighs the size and colour of hams. Gammon, we were. Bacon.

CAMILLE: And then before the rash from the venom reaching the lymph nodes had even faded, she'd upped sticks and taken herself off with that Mennonite.

ED: I thought he was Muslim.

CAMILLE: No, like the Osmonds. Not teeth – underwear.

ISABELLA: Mormon.

CAMILLE: You could see it, like a chastity belt, under his trousers, a little rib on each thigh where his *underthings* ended. Quite sexy really, made you want to touch it – you know, lean over and run your finger along… And they were at it like rabbits, apparently, day and night, but always through a hole in a sheet, or something.

ISABELLA: That's orthodox.

CAMILLE: Maybe it is to you young things nowadays, but I thought it was quite kinky, actually.

ISABELLA: Jew. Orthodox Jew. But it could be an urban myth? You know, anti-semite propaganda?

CAMILLE: And just when we thought she couldn't get any worse, there was the Sapphic era, the hairy God help us female ejaculation years.

ISABELLA: I'm still here.

ED: Not forgetting the car.

CAMILLE: Oh God! I'd almost succeeded in psychologically blocking out that whole episode.

ED: She went out with her car.

ISABELLA: Well, people usually do. That's how you get to where you're going.

ED: No, I mean dated.

ISABELLA: There's drive in movies and –

ED: – No – the car was her date. She fancied her car.

CAMILLE: She'd drive around in a high state of erotic excitement, and call it an *assignation*. Then she'd two-time her Honda Civic by waxing the neighbour's Mini. I tried to get her interested in valeting my VW, but she said it was too close to incest for comfort.

ED: 'Objectum sexuality.' I looked it up.

CAMILLE: Well I'd certainly object.

ED: At least she didn't get engaged to the Eiffel Tower. There was a documentary on the other night with this one diddling on the rails, claiming to be consummating the relationship. There she was on camera, rubbing away.

ISABELLA: You are aware I'm still in the room?

CAMILLE: We shouldn't mock the afflicted. I feel quite bad talking so disparagingly about you-know-who, as I think I formed her. I taught her to walk, you know.

ED: That was me.

CAMILLE: She was just a squashed face and a smelly, pissy nappy. No one took any interest in her.

ED: You're only eighteen months older.

CAMILLE: She'd just lie in the corner, talking to her toes, messing herself. No change there, then, from the last time I saw her.

ED: How could you teach her to walk when you could barely do it yourself?

CAMILLE: I used to take her favourite toy away – that horrendous sucky thing made out of a towelling sock –

ED: I gave her that.

CAMILLE: – and make her waddle towards me after it, force her to strive, to move out of the corner she was happy to lie in, like a pig in shit. Neglect. There'd be a court case if it happened nowadays.

Mother wasn't the most attentive of –

(ROSE enters.)

I have to say it's awfully warm in here.

ED: It's the exercise.

CAMILLE: Shifting a few chairs? I do yogilates three evenings a week, bums and tums boot camp every Saturday morning, plus my usual ten thousand steps a day. I've been chipped – had a pedometer embedded right here on my hipbone, counts every step and then sends the data to an app on my phone, brilliant. Then it calculates the daily strides and tells me if I need to run round the kitchen table a few times to reach my quota before going to bed.

ISABELLA: She's there sometimes until the middle of the night.

CAMILLE: That's a slight exaggeration. Anyway, with my regime carrying a chair from the middle of a room to the wall doesn't even register. It's simply hot in here.

ED: I don't know how. The heating's not on.

ROSE: We like a living temperature just south of the Arctic. There's nothing like seeing your frosty breath in the morning to confirm that unfortunately you made it through another night.

CAMILLE: But I'm boiling.

ROSE: You must be manufacturing your own seasons, darling. Never mind. It happens to the best of us, eventually.

CAMILLE: Oh God, is this how it starts?

ED: What?

CAMILLE: The beginning of the end. The change.

ISABELLA: I don't know.

CAMILLE: I'm melting.

ISABELLA: Well don't melt over me.

CAMILLE: I'm running with sweat.

ED: I believe you.

CAMILLE: Feel me.

ISABELLA: No.

CAMILLE: Go on.

ISABELLA: No.

CAMILLE: Look at my face then. Is it beaded? Beaded with sweat?

ISABELLA: That's gross.

CAMILLE: Oh my God, is this how it goes?

ED: Don't ask me.

CAMILLE: You're older than me.

ED: So?

CAMILLE: So you should have the change before me.

ED: Not necessarily.

CAMILLE: Bye bye babies.

ISABELLA: Now you're being weird.

CAMILLE: Bye-bye hormones. Hello sleepless nights, breasts pointing to the floor, rubbish hair.

That's it, then.

(She stands rigid, face contracting.)

ISABELLA: Are you okay? Your face has gone all…

CAMILLE: I'm concentrating.
Pelvic floor exercises.

ROSE: Must you, darling?

CAMILLE: Yes, I must.

ROSE: In here, where we eat? Surely it's not quite hygienic? And do we really have to talk about it? It wasn't done, in my day.

ED: Nothing was done in your day.

CAMILLE: We need to acknowledge these things, these rites of passage.
We need to rail against them, the dying of the light.

ROSE: You've probably got a touch of flu.

CAMILLE: Really?

ROSE: It wouldn't surprise me if you were running a temperature.

CAMILLE: You think so?

ROSE: Maybe it's an allergic reaction to all the decades of dust you've so efficiently put into the air.

CAMILLE: That might be it…

ROSE: Of course it is, darling. I've a feeling about it. Mummy knows best.
And that's an example of the kind of lies mothers are supposed to tell to help their children in some self-deception, so don't say I was never there for you.

The chairs are cleared. CAMILLE and ISABELLA begin rolling up the large rug, ED sweeping the floor with an industrial sized broom

(Of broom.) And pray where did that contraption come from?

CAMILLE: My car. Tools of the trade.

ROSE: How modern. My offspring is in *trade.*

CAMILLE: I've got wallpaper samples in the boot, and colour charts and –

ROSE: – If you're going to do this, I have to leave.

CAMILLE: I've a library of lovely design books – house and garden. I thought we could sit down and –

ROSE: – I can't bear all this hysterical cleaning and tidying up.

CAMILLE: We could compile some mood boards and –

ROSE: – You know I hate *improvement.* All the time and energy wasted on superficial activities that achieve nothing.

ED: Which of course you'd be uninterested in when there's so many other worthwhile things for you to do with your *endless* time.

ROSE: It's not endless. It's going to end. That's the point.

CAMILLE: And you're creating a home, a pleasant living environment. Some see it as an investment.

ROSE: One of the things that makes existence bearable is the certainty it's finite. You know my feelings on this.

ED: I do. And I think we have to –

ROSE: – We don't have to do anything.

ED: – sit down as a family and –

ROSE: – You do not dictate to me, you do not set my terms –

ED: – But –

ROSE: – No. And that's final.

(Beat.)

ISABELLA: Is everything okay?

ROSE: Is it a crime to want to leave the party early? I'm stone-cold sober, I don't like the music and there's no one to talk to.
And look at what you've done to the room! I was used to it as it was. It would've seen me out.

CAMILLE: Of course it wouldn't, you'll live to be ninety.

ROSE: *(Exiting.)* Dear God, no.

CAMILLE: And off she goes… and then she's gone.

ED: Story of my life. The closer I tried to get, the further Mother always seemed to be moving away.

They look where ROSE exited, absorbing.

ISABELLA: Is everything alright?

CAMILLE: Yes, munchkin.
(To ED.) Is it?

ED: I'm not saying anything until we're all together.

CAMILLE: Why not?

ED: I don't like repeating myself.

CAMILLE: It's Mother, isn't it, and the old complaint?

ED: Of course it's Mother. It's always Mother. Who else would it be but Mother?

CAMILLE: You.

ED: Me?

CAMILLE: Yes. You.

ED: Well it isn't. I'm fine. I'm busy.

CAMILLE: With what?

ED: My job.

CAMILLE: You're working? But that's great! What are you doing?

ED: Same as what I've always done. I'm a carer and a housekeeper. I care and keep house.

CAMILLE: But is that enough to keep you occupied, engaged? What about outside interests, activities…?
When did you last go away on holiday?

ED: You don't go away when you're keeping house. By definition my job is to stay still.

CAMILLE: But you've got to have a break…

ED: No.

CAMILLE: Get outside this house….?

ED: Not necessarily.

CAMILLE: Can you tell me the last place you visited outside these four walls?

ED: Yes, I could. But I choose not to.

ISABELLA: It was the supermarket.

ED: Nope. Home delivery. I shop on-line.

ISABELLA: The dentist's. Doctor's surgery?

CAMILLE: You need a bit of stimulus when you get to your age.

ED: You can travel without moving an atom. I can go anywhere inside my head. That's one place you can't control, one space you can't enter without my express invitation.

CAMILLE: Are you talking to me? I think you just jumped to a different conversation with another person – our sister, probably?

ED: No. I was talking to you, *Camomile.*

CAMILLE: *Camille.* The *om* is silent. It's like a meditation: Cam [om] ile.
I pronounce it 'Camille.'

ED: You might, but nobody else does. It's Camomile.

CAMILLE: No, it's –

ED: Named after the flower and the tea, otherwise known as Piss the Bed.

CAMILLE: I've been called Camille all my adult life, ever since I left this place, and I don't understand why, after thirty years –

ED: Forty.

CAMILLE: After thirty-two years –

ED: Thirty-eight.

CAMILLE: Why, after thirty-four years you can't respect how I wish to self-identify and call me the name I have chosen and am known by.

ED: But your name's Camomile, Piss the Bed.

CAMILLE: It was, but is no longer. It says Camille on my passport.

ED: Is that the passport that has 'Employment: fashion model'?

CAMILLE: That was a mistake, a clerical error thirty years ago and I wondered how long it would take to get started… the humiliation, this constant attempt to destroy my self-esteem. Well I won't accept it. You can't belittle me. You can only make me feel small if I give my permission and I do not give it. I will not feel small I will not feel small I feel so small. *(To ISABELLA.)* Now do you understand why I hate coming here?

ISABELLA: I quite like 'Camomile.'

CAMILLE: Do you?

ISABELLA: It's kind of –

CAMILLE: – cool?

ISABELLA: No.

CAMILLE: No, of course it wouldn't be *cool*… Funky?

ISABELLA: Not exactly.

CAMILLE: Then what?

ISABELLA: Give me a minute.

Knocking at the door, off. ISABELLA moves to answer as MAUREEN appears.

MAUREEN: No. I'll get it.

She crosses, interminably slow, an assault course around the moved chairs.
The doorbell rings.

ISABELLA: Can I – ?

MAUREEN: No. It's for me. I'm to get it.

Another knock.

ISABELLA: But I could –

MAUREEN: Patience is a virtue.

(Calling.) Don't get your knickers in a twist; I'm on my way!

She finally crosses. Off, the door opens and then immediately slams shut. After a moment, the doorbell rings.

CAMILLE: What the – ?

ED: Leave it.

Loud knocking of the morally superior variety. The door is finally opened.

MAUREEN: *(Off.)* She doesn't want to see you. She told you that, after the last time. It's not compulsory, she hasn't been sectioned, you have no right of access and if you persist, this could be see as trespass and aggravation, so do us all a favour will you, and feck off?

Resounding door slam. MAUREEN and ROSE come in together.

ROSE: I was hiding behind the coat stand, ready to lift a walking stick to protect myself, if need be. Thank you. You were magnificent! You're the only one who does anything for me. Thank you so much for standing up to her. Especially after that last appointment!

CAMILLE: What's going on?

ROSE: Such a load of… 'You should dress yourself in purple,' she said 'and spend all your money on jam or caviar

CAMILLE: Hello?

ROSE: 'and not pay bills and wear rainbow wellies and go splashing about in puddles and never mind it is raining, see instead the angels crying.

CAMILLE: Who's she talking about?

ROSE: 'Think of strangers as friends you haven't met yet and that a mother holds her child's hand for a while but their heart forever

ED: Her geriatric psychiatrist.

ROSE: 'and indulge yourself with clashing violets and mauve marabou mules and not wearing any underwear.'

CAMILLE: Her what?

ROSE: And I said 'where the fuck did you get that from? Oh, sorry, did I surprise you, being a curser, a blasphemer and profanity maker? Did I shock you by swearing, by using a very naughty word?'

MAUREEN: It always does shock them, though I don't know why. Do you become lesser, or more kind, just because your body's ready to disintegrate?

CAMILLE: Gertiatric –?

ISABELLA: – Psychiatrist. I think they just denied entry to Granny's mental health visitor.

CAMILLE: Right!

CAMILLE grabs her coat and heads out the front door

ROSE: And 'no', she said, 'I'm improvising on a theme. I thought it might inspire you, help get you away from the glums.'

ED: 'The glums'?!

ROSE: 'It's a poem,' she said, 'the nation's favourite poem, about ageing and getting old. And as you have the ageing glums, I thought it might be helpful to extemporise on the theme.' 'Which really,' I said, 'is about wearing purple.' 'Yes, I suppose it is,' she simpered – I'm sorry, but it's the only word for it: she *simpered*. 'Well, as you can see from the thread veins on my face,' I told her, 'purple is not my colour.'
And now I'm spoilt!

MAUREEN: You are not!

ROSE: I am, just look at me!

MAUREEN: You've hardly changed!

ROSE: Do you think so? Bless you! As if I'd believe that! But bless your heart. Bless your craven heart. But now I'm ruined! Don't look at me, don't don't don't.

ED: *(To ISABELLA.)* I like to be near people.

ROSE: I used to be quite a looker in my time. Nothing to write home about – well, maybe a postcard.

ED: *(To ISABELLA.)* I don't like to be alone.

ROSE: I'm eighty-two, you know. Remarkable for my age, aren't I?

MAUREEN: Especially as you're seventy-six.

ISABELLA: Why does she do that? Add years? Wish her life away?

ED: It's the walls. They close in.

ROSE: I have been known to turn the odd head.

ED: I get afraid. So terribly afraid…

It hangs in the air. Finally:

ROSE: Of what, you goose?

ED: It all.
Afraid the phone will ring. Afraid it won't. Scared someone will come and want to talk to me – like those consumer questionnaire people.

ROSE: I pray a consumer questionnaire person will come and ask me to fill out a form. Then I'd tell them what for.

ED: Or be asked to sample something – some instant non-calorie hot chocolate, or reconstituted chicken meat, or shampoo. A new brand of margarine… I'd be brave and do it loyally and promptly, truthfully – I wouldn't shirk my duty – I'd get a special pen and record all my thoughts and reactions down on the sheet, tick the box, continue onto another sheet of paper, if necessary. And be thanked for it. Be an expert, one of those surveyed. To be someone whose opinions count.

MAUREEN: The day I stopped worrying what everyone else thought of me was the day I realised nobody listened, anyway.

ED: I've become the atheist who prays. The things we do for comfort – to be out of fear.

ISABELLA: I'm not afraid. I'd rather face cold hard reality full-on than be drugged with some false belief system.

MAUREEN: Hear the baby talk!

ROSE: Hear the angels sing!

ISABELLA: Please don't patronise me.

ROSE: I assure you I was not. I was admiring, warming my cold hands on the furnace of your idealism.

MAUREEN: It can be cold and lonely, sometimes.

ED: And it gets colder.

MAUREEN: When you're just a skinbag of bones, you can be grateful for a little cushioning.

ISABELLA: Even if we're lying to ourselves?

ROSE: That's the girl! Tell it as it is.

ED: The glass is half empty rather than half full? It's a good and dignified death to cut life off in its prime?

ROSE: In my opinion, for what it's worth, it's better not to think of the bloody glass at all, but savour the sweetness of the liquid within.

ISABELLA: But it's all interpretation, isn't it? Not real, just states of mind.

ED: Do you ever watch your hand on the steering wheel when driving – 10 to 2 – one inch one way or another could completely alter the course of your life and the kids in the back of the approaching car coming home on the school run. Just an inch – one way or another… Have you ever felt that?

ISABELLA: I don't drive.

ED: Neither do I.

ROSE: *(To ISABELLA.)* You'll learn.

ED: I don't even go out. I meant it as an example... I meant… Have you never felt that desperation – the slow asphyxiation of the soul…?

ISABELLA: No.

ED: Are you sure?

ISABELLA: Yes.

ED: It's real, in the body, not my head.

ROSE: Goose! You do create… There's nothing special about you. We all get fearful, we all get depressed.

ED: She doesn't.

ROSE: She just doesn't recognise it, yet. She thinks it's a hangover or period pain, and not typical existential angst.

MAUREEN: We all get it.

ISABELLA: I don't.

ED: She doesn't.

ROSE: She's lying.

ISABELLA: I'm not. I'm pathologically unable to lie.

ROSE: You're young. You will, trust me. And there's nothing wrong with feeling down –

ISABELLA: – Excuse me, but…

ROSE: No, dear. I'm sorry. Sometimes the grown-ups really do know best. Just sit there and try to be decorative, for once in your young life, if it isn't too much of a challenge for you.
Right?
Lovely.
There's nothing wrong with feeling down. Despair is a natural human condition. It's what separates us from the beasts. I mean, have you ever seen a depressed penguin?

ISABELLA: I knew a suicidal dog. And I think all Labradors are bipolar. All that crazed tail wagging and silly grins and melting eyes… Have you seen one when it's naughty or sulking, or overcome with guilt for something it may or may not have done? They're pathological. And cats…! Sociopaths! Such nasty, manipulative, selfish things. At least dogs are faithful. A dog wouldn't make a meal of you if you died locked in a sad bedsit, but a cat would. And come back for seconds.

ROSE: It's really quite extraordinary, isn't it…?

ISABELLA: What?

MAUREEN: You just destroyed her complete hypothesis.

ISABELLA: Did I? Oh, sorry.

ROSE: Not to worry, dear.

ISABELLA: Sorry! My mother always says I should check my mind is in operation before I put my mouth into gear.

ROSE: Does she really?

ED: Your mother.

ISABELLA: Yes.

ED: Is she ill yet?

ISABELLA: 'Yet'?!

MAUREEN: Ssssh.

ISABELLA: 'Yet'?!

ROSE: Well, we always do, don't we, darling? We get ill and recover, ill and recover, ill until one day we don't recover…

ISABELLA: 'Yet'?!

ED: Just wondering how she is…

ISABELLA: She's very well, thank you. In perfect health. You've seen her yourself. You can ask her!

ED: Get her to check that little… *(Stops.)*

MAUREEN: Don't.

ISABELLA: What?

ROSE: Yes, don't.

ED: That little *(She coughs genteelly.)*

MAUREEN: Pay no attention.

ISABELLA: What? What?!

ROSE: You shouldn't do this.

ISABELLA: Don't, please – don't start and then… Look, if you know something about Mam I should know, please… this is… Please…

ED: *(Low.)* Can you feel it?
Can you? Can you?

ISABELLA: I…

ED: Feel that grip, right in the gut…?
Sense that fist clenching – fingers tightening around your heart, restricting the beat – pum-pa-pum-pa-pum-pa-pa-pum-pa-pa-pa-pa-pum…it gets out of sync, amplified, in your ears… squeezed… can you feel it?

ISABELLA: Yes.

ED: Do you know what it is?

ISABELLA: The thing that's wrong with my mother?

ED: Do you know what it is?

ISABELLA: No.

ED: That's low level panic, the seed of fear. And when it flowers, you have despair. So now you know what it's like.

ROSE: That wasn't very nice.

ED: Didn't see you trying to stop me.

ISABELLA: Oh! You –

ROSE: I did try.

MAUREEN: Not very hard.

ROSE: Her mother reckons she needs toughening up a bit.

ISABELLA: That was so…

ED: I try to cry. I sit myself down and say 'right! You're going to do this! Have a good mourn and cry. Let it all out.' But it won't come.

ISABELLA: You…

ED: So now we're all the same. We have a shared vocabulary. We can communicate. You say tomato and I say tomato. I talk about slow asphyxiation of the soul and you have a glimmer of what I'm talking about.

ISABELLA: That was… horrible. You didn't need to…

ED: Have a cry if you can. It's very good for you. Let it all out – the nightmares, clear the sinuses, sleep easy at night – and whatever happens, do not be like me. Do not turn out like me.

A woman dressed in loose, layered clothing enters, her head swathed in cloth.

GLORIA: The door was open, so I –

They stare.

Hello, everyone.
(To ROSE.) Hello, Mummy.
My, doesn't this look cosy?

End of scene.

THREE

A short time after. CAMILLE has just returned, arms filled with curtain swatches, colour charts, a heavy thick book of carpet samples and other paraphernalia from the boot of her car. The others are sitting on furniture in an arrangement almost resembling a social domestic space. It is a cosy oasis in a desert of emptiness.

CAMILLE: *(Of GLORIA.)* What's that on her head?

ED: Her hair.

CAMILLE: No. The – *(She gestures.)*

GLORIA: It's a kind of zukin – a head-covering? I'll take it off if it's distracting. We don't have to wear it.

She removes it from her head.

ROSE: 'We' darling?

GLORIA: Yes. It's more symbolic really, an outward sign of the inner commitment.

ROSE: To…?

GLORIA: Ourselves. The truth.

ED: Of course.

GLORIA: To person-centred care.

ROSE: So it's a sort of hospice where you volunteer?

GLORIA: It's a community, really. It's – home.

ROSE: I see.

GLORIA: There was a time when people used to care. Now, it's a profession. We're so industrialised in our looking after one another, so processed and medicalised, we've lost the simplicity, the connection of just being. We're so far from life and death and the natural and the real. Our comings and goings are managed, sanitised, delayed, prolonged, speeded-up, made inhuman. Our processes, our life itself, it's…

ROSE: Yes?

GLORIA: …Divorced from us. And we're separate from each other.

CAMILLE: What's that on her head?

ED: Her hair.

CAMILLE: No it's not, it's –
(To ED.) Ask her what she's done to her hair.
(To ISABELLA.) Ask her what she –

ISABELLA: – Ask her yourself.

GLORIA: And our doctors are taught to solve and mend as though we're immortal and can always get better. We can't. We're *supposed* to have a 'best before' date; we've been designed to expire. We're organic matter, not Teflon. And so that natural pause, the final full stop has been ostracised –

ROSE: Precisely.

GLORIA: – moved from the centre of the family to being outsourced, just another unpleasant job someone else can deal with without inconveniencing us too much.

CAMILLE: What's that on her –

GLORIA: – It's my hair. Okay?

CAMILLE: What's she done to it?

GLORIA: I'm speaking.

CAMILLE: But it used to be all nasty and carroty and

GLORIA: I used to henna it, but I've stopped all that now.

CAMILLE: It's silver.

ROSE: It's called ageing.

CAMILLE: It used to be.

GLORIA: Hennaed, yes. A lovely, safe vegetable dye. Brought out the natural colour of my hair.

CAMILLE: It wasn't her natural colour. She was mouse-brown.

GLORIA: With auburn highlights.

CAMILLE: My arse. She had that flat, dull nothing colour hair. Absorbed light, didn't reflect it, like a rat. It was rat brown. Auburn my –

GLORIA: – Natural remedies merely enhance what is naturally there.

CAMILLE: Says who? And it wasn't natural full stop. It was too bright. And shiny. And chemically. And false.

GLORIA: It was herbal.

CAMILLE: Is that what you call it?

ED: It's gone now, so it doesn't matter!

ISABELLA: And anyway, everybody does it, even our ancestors. In archaeology club I saw this documentary about the Caucasoids of the Tarim Basin, third century BC.

ROSE: Good grief. I believe she's swallowed an encyclopaedia.

ISABELLA: There was a man found with red hennaed hair and this awesome sunburst design tattooed on his temple.

CAMILLE: I don't hold with needles and ink, mutilating yourself in the name of fashion.

ISABELLA: But it isn't, can't you see? It's elemental, part of human nature. I was thinking of getting it done on my shoulder blade.

CAMILLE: What?

ISABELLA: The tattoo. Just small, on my shoulder, so it's not visible all the time, but there, for me to know…

CAMILLE: Excuse us for a moment…

(Takes ISABELLA aside, but everyone can still hear.)

If you *dare* vandalise that beautiful skin… If you dare ruin that skin I spent so long growing and nurturing and not just when I was carrying you and eating all the food I hated and the vitamin E and B supplements which repeated and gave me heartburn just to give you perfect, unblemished skin, but since you were born – the diet of organic food three times the price of normal veg' and the overtime I did to pay for it, so you wouldn't be tormented with acne and being called craterface. And that's not even mentioning the so-called relaxing holidays ruined by the continual wrestling bouts to get sunscreen on you or a hat tied under your chin and the CARE, this constant, loving *care*… Do you think I did all that so you could graffiti this work of art just because you felt like it? I didn't do all that so you could deface your skin on a whim you'll regret by the time you're twenty when you see your so-called individualism is just joining the herd, moo! Joining the others with their tramp stamp vandalism and meaningless aphorisms scored in unintelligible vertical languages in places where there shouldn't be print. I'm telling you, if you get a tattoo, I'm telling you now, if you do, I'll cut it off. I'll get a big sharp knife and I'll hold you down and I'll

GLORIA: I don't know what the fuss is about.

ED: What's that?

GLORIA: I said I don't know what the all singing and dancing's about.

CAMILLE: Oh.

Don't you.

GLORIA: The hoo-ha, given the other sorrows and issues in the world.

CAMILLE: If I want to know what you think, I'll ask you, okay?

GLORIA: Okay.

ROSE: Girls…

GLORIA: And I acknowledge your hostility. It's understandable. Families are rigid structures;

they don't want evolution. They want to keep you in your unhappy, unrealised place.

CAMILLE: When I want your opinion, I'll invite interaction.

GLORIA: Sure.

CAMILLE: When I want an uninformed opinion from someone who never reared a child, indeed, never even had a conversation with one in their entire life if memory serves me right, not even a chat with their supposed Godchild – abandoned at the font before the holy water dried if truth be told.

ISABELLA: It's fine.

CAMILLE: *(To ISABELLA.)* It's not. *(To GLORIA.)* Let me assure you, if I want that, you'll be the first I'll ask.

GLORIA: Thanks. And that's great practise, you know.

CAMILLE: What.

GLORIA: It's healthy not to keep everything buttoned up. Repression causes strokes.

CAMILLE: And there's me thinking it was hardening of the arteries and related problems.

GLORIA: But what causes the problems? Stress. Cynicism. Sarcasm. Unhappiness.

CAMILLE: No. We are not going to have the conversation about unhappiness. Mother – if she begins on that conversation, I swear I will kill her.

ROSE: Why are you all looking at me?

GLORIA: We have to be open to what life's trying to teach us.

CAMILLE: I will put my hands around her throat and squeeze and squeeze and squeeze… .

ROSE: You're all grown-up.

CAMILLE: Or I'll ransack the kitchen drawers and try to find some instrument sharp enough to puncture her lungs but blunt enough not to kill her immediately so she can see my little dance of victory for remaining in the world as she is leaving it.

ED: Mother?

ROSE: You can deal with her yourselves.

CAMILLE: Or I'll suffocate her with a pillow –

ISABELLA: Mam… .

CAMILLE: with my own backside, if need be – I'll *sit* her to death.

ROSE: And to think I taught her how to walk and talk… .

ED: I think you'll find that was me.

ISABELLA: Mam, can I ask just one thing?

CAMILLE: Or just squash her – flatten her like an ant – no, a cockroach –

ISABELLA: *(Overlapping.)* Mam… Look at me. MAM?!

(CAMILLE stops and looks.)

Didn't you do the same when you were younger?

CAMILLE: What's that, munchkin?

ISABELLA: Didn't you experiment with styles and appearances? Colour of hair? When you were younger?

CAMILLE: No.

GLORIA: Yes.

CAMILLE: No.

ED: Oh, yes.

CAMILLE: NO I DIDN'T.

ED&GLORIA: YES SHE DID.

CAMILLE: They never had colour like that when I was younger.

ROSE: Oh, of course, it was all sepia then, wasn't it, darling? And empire line dresses and leg o' mutton sleeves and pig in a poke bonnets.

As they speak MAUREEN enters, stops, goes out, comes back in again, looks, can't recognise where she is, gets confused, then eventually realises it is the right room and begins passing through to the garden.

GLORIA: I'm sorry that something as insignificant as my hair has caused such interest and controversy in your oh my goodness shallow lives. I had no idea.

GLORIA notices MAUREEN and becomes fixated on her, rather as CAMILLE was on first meeting.

ED: And if she wants a tattoo, let her.

GLORIA: *(Of MAUREEN.)* Isn't anyone going to introduce us?

ROSE: Yes, it's her body. It seems to me she should be allowed to do what she wants with it.

ED: Oh, here we go....

ROSE: Surely it's the one thing we actually own in this world – the physical substance of our self – so by rights we should be able to do whatever we like with it.

GLORIA: Within reason.

CAMILLE: But a tattoo....

ROSE: I was thinking of having one done myself. On my chest. Declaring my intentions to the world.

CAMILLE: Mother, don't be so ridiculous.

ROSE: Ridiculous is it? It's life and death to some.

ROSE opens the neck of her blouse to reveal printed across her sternum DO NOT RESUSCITATE.

Do not resuscitate.
I decline further investigation and intervention.
I decline antibiotics if I get pneumonia.

MAUREEN joins in, like mumbling a catechism.

MAUREEN: & ROSE: I decline being kept alive by artificial means.
I decline hospitalisation.
I wish to die in my own bed.

A beat.

ISABELLA: I think it's eyebrow pencil.

MAUREEN: Felt tip. We were having a dry run.

CAMILLE: *(To MAUREEN.)* And I suppose this is your idea?

MAUREEN: Oh no, for me, it's the opposite. I'm going to have: 'Keep Me Alive Even Against Your Better Judgement.' When you're not the usual meat and two veg, shelf life can be a real problem. There's always some chancer wanting to be compassionate and help you out of your misery. If it were up to others, I'd've been put down years ago… The trick is to keep moving.

CAMILLE: Exactly. And along we go, nothing to see here. The garden and its carnivorous flowers is that way.

(MAUREEN slowly continues towards the garden.)

What on earth is going on Mother?

ROSE: My wishes.
I've never forgiven myself for what happened to your father. He wouldn't have wanted every Tom, Dick, or Harry poking and prodding and doing procedures to prolong his life when we all knew he was done for. They should have sewn him up and sent him

home, not keep picking and pulling at him, like crows on a dying lamb in a field. It was a horrible end of life. No dignity, no peace.

GLORIA: And that's what we're trying to change through our work at the hospice. We also consider the spiritual, psychological and emotional needs of a person nearing the end of their life. Hospital's a machine, and your husband, or your daughter, or your father, or *you* just become a medical problem to be solved.

MAUREEN: A breathing sudoku.
When they see you as a puzzle and not a person – just ticking meat – that's when it's time to get out, and fast.

ROSE: I'm taking no risks. There'll be no doubt about my intentions. I'll make an advance decision, signed and witnessed and legally binding, and an appointed power of attorney outside the family.

CAMILLE: *Outside*?

ROSE: Whom else should I use? A solicitor who doesn't know the first thing about me?

ED: One of us?

CAMILLE: Me?

ROSE: Oh don't be ridiculous darling. I'd want to choose someone who had my interests and not theirs at heart. She won't get a penny.

MAUREEN: Not a penny. *Dim money-o.*

(She exits into garden.)

CAMILLE: Her?!

ROSE: She's just doing it to be useful. She'll put my welfare first.

GLORIA: And you're saying we wouldn't?

ROSE: Of course not darling. You'd want your own wishes, not mine.

GLORIA: That's not true.

MAUREEN interrupts as she immediately re-enters and starts crossing.

MAUREEN: In the garden. My mother's good chairs, out there, in the garden. Would you call that gratitude?

ROSE: Oh, darling, don't take it to heart. It's the girls. You know how much they bully me.

GLORIA: Mother?

ROSE: They get together and gang up on me, do whatever they like. I told them to leave it be

CAMILLE: Mam.

ROSE: but I might as well have been talking to the wall for all the attention they paid. It was the same when they were young. Strength in numbers.

She follows MAUREEN out.

CAMILLE: Who is she, this…?

ED: Mother's – helper? She came back with her one day from the hospital.

GLORIA: She's very nice in her own way I'm sure, clearly battling with her self-actualisation, but nevertheless –

CAMILLE: There's a stranger about, an unknown woman in my house.

ED: Well, technically it's Mother's house.

CAMILLE: And when I say *my* house, I mean *our* house.

GLORIA: It's the family home. The nest.

CAMILLE: Father's nest egg, our inheritance. And there's a stranger in our midst. We have no idea who this woman is.

GLORIA: And Mother is reaching that time in her life when she

CAMILLE: might want to downsize

GLORIA: could be deceived

CAMILLE: yes

GLORIA: duped into signing away

CAMILLE: what should be ours

GLORIA: her soul

CAMILLE: right

GLORIA: because she's vulnerable and unhappy and completely hollow

because she has nothing in her life to give it any meaning.

ED: She's got us.

GLORIA: No moral compass, no spiritual well-being, no sense of anything greater outside her narrow self.

CAMILLE: She's got a granddaughter. The next generation.

GLORIA: She has nothing.

ED: I'm here.

GLORIA: And a fat lot of good you've been.

CAMILLE: Yeah. You let that woman move in.

ED: She's Mother's friend!

CAMILLE: You opened the door to heaven knows what –

ED: They like each other!

GLORIA: And you know what happens when people get older…

ISABELLA: They gain wisdom and experience.

CAMILLE: No, they get addled and confused, ripe for exploitation.

ED: Mother is as sharp as she's ever been. Sharper, if anything.

CAMILLE: And the state of the place when I arrived! I thought you were 'the housekeeper'?

ED: That's how she wanted it!

CAMILLE: An absolute health hazard, not to mention a wilful depreciation of the value of the property. Anyone would think you were doing it on purpose.

GLORIA: It wouldn't surprise me.

CAMILLE: Not that you have a say in the matter. You don't live here.

GLORIA: Neither do you.

CAMILLE: In fact, I can't remember the last time you visited.

ED: Ditto to both of you.

GLORIA: We're here now, isn't that enough?

ED: No it isn't. You have no idea… no idea either of you what it's like to live here.

GLORIA: So move out if it's such a hardship.

CAMILLE: Yeah. Don't try to guilt trip us about your own choices.

GLORIA: We didn't make you stay here.

CAMILLE: Exactly.

GLORIA: So go.

CAMILLE: Yeah, go on.

ED: And leave her alone?

GLORIA: She's got her 'companion.'

CAMILLE: It's like a social experiment dreamt up by Josef Mengele: leave a mad woman and her dubious sidekick together and see what mess they get into.

ISABELLA: You're getting offensive.

CAMILLE: Liberalism gone mad! Let the inmates take over the asylum –

GLORIA: – Our mother is not an inmate and neither is there anything wrong with her faculties.

CAMILLE: Oh, and you'd know!

ED: Here we go…

GLORIA: She's simply lost in a spiritual desert –

CAMILLE: – which you'd know all about seeing you're here so often. In fact, we can't get you to stay away!

GLORIA: I can't talk to you when you get like this.

CAMILLE: Like what?

GLORIA: This.

CAMILLE: And what exactly is 'this'?

GLORIA: You know.

CAMILLE: No, I don't.

GLORIA: Oh come on!

CAMILLE: I assure you I don't. Why would I say otherwise?

GLORIA: Because you would.

CAMILLE: Would what?

GLORIA: Act like this!

CAMILLE: Which is –?

GLORIA: You're doing it!

CAMILLE: What?

GLORIA: This!

CAMILLE: What am I doing?

GLORIA: *This!*

CAMILLE: What?!

GLORIA: This! *This!* You're doing *this!*

CAMILLE: Well that was illuminating. Look, you for one may want to spend all night screeching like a banshee and scoring points, but I don't. You may not care about our Mother, but I for one –

GLORIA: – How dare you! How dare you even imply that I don't care – very deeply – about our Mother and her welfare!

ISABELLA: We know you care. Of course you care.

GLORIA: Is it the old complaint? Has the condition accelerated? Is that why you called me?

ISABELLA: No.

GLORIA: Then why is she talking about living wills? I thought the doctor said the condition had plateaued and was stable.

ED: He did say that three years ago when you last bothered to check in.

GLORIA: Don't start.

CAMILLE: Yes, not now.

ED: Fine.

GLORIA: Has there been a deterioration? I know it's progressive and degenerative, but

GLORIA & CAMILLE: She could live to be ninety.

GLORIA: And no matter what you say, she's not mad.

CAMILLE: So how do you explain what she wants to do? How else do you explain this stupid idea she's got into her head if it's not delusional behaviour, or the first signs of dementia, or –

GLORIA: What exactly are you going on about?

ED: Our Mother wants to kill herself.

CAMILLE: Yes. I spoke with her psychiatrist.

ED: And not only that, she wants somebody to help.

ISABELLA: So the question is: do we let a stranger assist, or do we help her?

ED: What?!

CAMILLE: No! That isn't the question!

ISABELLA: Isn't it?

GLORIA: Did she just say what I thought she said?

ISABELLA: I thought that was what we were here to discuss. Well, *one* of the things. Mam wanted to –

CAMILLE: – Not now.

ED: Go on.

CAMILLE: No, we're fine. Let's proceed.

ED: No, I'd really like to know 'what Mam wanted…'

GLORIA: Excuse me? Isn't the focus shifting – as per usual? This always happens. You've got such a talent for this – always have to be the centre, the main protagonist of whatever drama is spinning out around you. I've had a lifetime of it. Being in your shadow, never being the focal point, not able to get in two words around your –

ISABELLA: – Weren't we talking about Granny?

GLORIA: And oh! Like mother, like daughter. You trained her well.

ISABELLA: We were talking about my Grandmother, your Mother, and whether to assist her in her suicide and

GLORIA: How can you –!? I for one believe in the sanctity of life, its preciousness. And I won't breathe the same air as those who even contemplate… I can't even say it. I'm having nothing to do with any of this. I can't even be in the same room. The iron is entering the soul.

GLORIA leaves. They look at each other.

CAMILLE: She is so like Mother.

End of scene.

FOUR

ISABELLA, ROSE and ED are surrounded by books, which ISABELLA occasionally reads aloud from. CAMILLE is redecorating, painting the walls. A makeover is in progress, the room beginning to be transformed.

ISABELLA: *(Reading.) Exsanguination.* This method attempts to self-inflict a class IV haemorrhage by traumatic bleeding. The technique –

CAMILLE: – The trouble with old houses is whether to go all Inigo Jones Vitruvian rules of proportion and symmetry, or candy floss baroque Esther Williams.

ED: Wasn't she the synchronised Hollywood swimmer?

ROSE: *(To ISABELLA.)* Go on.

CAMILLE: *Bunny.* I meant *Bunny* Williams, the American interior designer.

ISABELLA: *(Reading.)* The technique may be performed with a single or multiple incisions

CAMILLE: Is it age?

ISABELLA: and/or lacerations at wrists.

CAMILLE: I feel like I've been rewired –

ISABELLA: The radial artery, ulner artery, cephalic vein and basilica vein are obvious candidates.

CAMILLE: – the plug's gone into the wrong socket.

ED: Said the actress to the bishop.

CAMILLE: I've all the relevant information, just occasionally can't call it up; or it gets confused: Martha becomes Arthur, Wittgenstein becomes Frankenstein.

ISABELLA: *(Reading.)* The victim–

ROSE: – Heroine, please.

ISABELLA: – will experience a drop in blood pressure, increased heart rate, somatic pain and peripheral perfusion.

ROSE: I don't like the sound of that.

CAMILLE: Why is ageing worse for women than men?

ROSE: When I go, I want to slip off quietly, not like I'm on a rollercoaster ride.

ISABELLA: But that'd be awesome – a completely original way to go – just undo your safety belt on the triple loop.

ED: They're no longer manually operated. I checked.

CAMILLE: We have to bear all the insults of temporary memory loss, hot flushes, loss of libido, vaginal dryness –

ISABELLA: I'm still in the room.

CAMILLE: – whilst men get all distinguished and crinkly and silver foxy and strangely sexy.

ROSE: What else?

ISABELLA: Drowning?

CAMILLE: It shouldn't be *Mother* Nature – unless she hates her gender.

ED: Or her offspring.

CAMILLE: Maybe that's it –

ISABELLA: Accounts for less than 2% of all reported suicides.

CAMILLE: – she hates her female offspring.

ROSE: I hear it's very soothing. Therapeutic almost. A minute's thrashing about in the water, then an eternity of being serene. None of that being found on the bathroom floor with your knickers around your ankles in a pool of your own unmentionables like poor old Elvis.

ED: Nope. We're unsinkable. Family trait. It's like we have styrofoam skulls, just keep bobbing up to the surface.

ISABELLA: Not if you have concrete boots.

ED: And where would we get them?

ISABELLA: You can outsource anything nowadays. Or you could just hire someone to do it.

ROSE: But then it would be murder, which defeats the whole purpose.

ISABELLA: No it doesn't. If you wanted to be dead, you'd be dead. What's the difference?

ROSE: The route of getting there.

ED: So how is having someone assist you different from taking out a contract on your life?

ROSE: The violent means and paying an assassin.

ISABELLA: But isn't death always violent – what it *does* – what it *means*?

CAMILLE: Why are we having this morbid conversation?

ROSE: You agreed to acknowledge the elephant in the room if I agreed we sit down like reasonable people and find other ways of apparently being active whilst still skirting the whole issue.

ISABELLA: No, it's research. It's useful.

ROSE: It's just skating around the edges, pretending to talk whilst actually avoiding the whole conversation. Which is: When I choose, at a certain point in the swiftly approaching future, I want to be assisted in putting out the light.

CAMILLE: You can't even talk about it, except in romantic literary euphemisms! Mother, you are not Desdemona!

ISABELLA: What we're doing is considering the options.

ED: And paving the way for a lovely long stretch in prison.

CAMILLE: You do know what you're asking is illegal?

ROSE: What did I ask of you, exactly?

(Beat.)

Nothing.

ISABELLA: And we're just talking about it. Nobody's doing anything.

CAMILLE: But it's not like you're unable to swallow pills and throw a bottle of booze down your throat without help. Why involve other people?

ROSE: I'm concerned I'll do it wrong. I'd get myself all psyched up and ready to compost and then wake up, with the weight of those head-shrinkers and muesli knitters hanging around my neck and no chance to get my hands on any strong drugs for the foreseeable future. And then I'd be trapped, in an increasingly mutinous body that refuses to do what I ask of it.

ED: But you're not at that stage yet, if ever.

ROSE: Age will get me, either way. It's all down hill from here on. This is as good as it gets, the pinnacle. I don't want to go into decline.

CAMILLE: But why involve someone else? Are you sure it isn't sheer idleness? Mother – be truthful. Are you really so lazy you can't even organise your own suicide, but want someone to come round and do it for you?

ED: It's not dial-a-death, like ordering a pizza. 'Would that be with the strychnine base and extra hemlock on top?'

CAMILLE: 'We're doing a special, today. Buy one and get the family sized potassium chloride cheesy stuffed crust half price.'

ROSE: Oh, you're so droll. Just go back to your insipid, mindless homemaking and leave us to get on with the business of dying, please.

CAMILLE: I'll have you know interior decoration is deeply theoretical.

ROSE: I'm sure it is, dear. All that matching cushions with wallpaper must give Grothendieck's Galois theory a run for its money.

MAUREEN enters, crossing slowly towards the garden to empty her catheter.

ED: Is there a way of assisting without knowing you're assisting?

CAMILLE: Now that really is wishful thinking.

ISABELLA: *(Finding reference in book.)* They call it 'suicide by cop' in America. You provoke an armed officer into using lethal force, or you commit a capital offence in the hope of being sentenced to death.

MAUREEN: And then sit on death row for ten years, with some *twpsyn* wanting to marry you, or campaigning so you don't get the fatal injection…

ISABELLA: *(Reading from book.)* 'It's setting out on an obviously fatal course, like becoming a solider –

CAMILLE: – Or smoking, so don't start.

ISABELLA: '– but without directly committing the act upon oneself. State assisted suicide was very popular in the Enlightenment era

Scandinavia, where the law and religion forbade suicide.'

ED: So what are they going to do? Imprison your corpse?

ISABELLA: It's damning your eternal soul – committing it to Hell forever. And Buddhists believe that, too.

ED: So convert to Islam and be promised a seat in heaven and 77 virgins, or whatever it is.

MAUREEN: Sounds like a rugby song.

(Sings.) 'One and twenty virgins went off to Inverness,
And when they returned there was one and twenty less.'

ROSE: The pity is none of you are aware of how inappropriate that is.

CAMILLE: Said she who's encouraging her grandchild to browse through the *Encyclopaedia of Self-Destruction.*

ROSE: It's educational.

ISABELLA: I don't mind.

CAMILLE: Maybe I do.

ISABELLA: So? You're not me.

CAMILLE: Oh no?

ISABELLA: We were separated at birth. Once the umbilical was cut, I was me and you continued to be you. We were never the same person, anyway. You were just the host.

CAMILLE: Excuse me?

ISABELLA: And I was a parasitic growth that got cut out of you. Don't look to me to romanticise it. I mean, my Dad came from a wank bottle.

ED: So it hasn't been the most meaningful of relationships?

ISABELLA: Hi Dad, the specimen jar…

ROSE: Isn't there a more dignified way of doing away with yourself?

ISABELLA: *(Reading.)* Apocarteresis?

ROSE: I like the sound of that.

ISABELLA: Suicide by starvation.

ED: There's hundreds in rest homes and geriatric wards dying of malnutrition. I saw it on telly. They just stop eating.

ROSE: The final act of protest, the last resort to try and be in control.

MAUREEN: But not every hunger strike is by choice. Some need help with the fork and spoon, or can't reach the plate banged down just a few inches out of range. I'm not saying it's intentional – but the results are the same. *(Exiting into garden.)*

ROSE: Which is why I intend to checkout before having to face that kind of eventuality.

ISABELLA: It's like the children's euthanasia project in Germany in the 1930's – death from hunger or thirst rather than waste an injection. Well, that was before they perfected the gas ovens on them, of course, and we all know where that ended…

CAMILLE: How on earth do you know all this?

ISABELLA: The extra-curricular class you enrolled me on during spring half term break.

CAMILLE: I was working.

ROSE: Are you never *not*?

MAUREEN re-enters pushing in one of the wing chairs from the garden before her.

CAMILLE: I want her to be independent and polished, everything I wasn't at her age. And some psychologists believe it can be positively damaging to be tied to your mother's apron strings.

ED: Though personally, it would have been nice to experience that: apron strings, closeness, attention, not being ignored all the time.

ROSE: Is that a complaint, darling? Do I ascertain a little criticism there in your words?

ISABELLA: *(Referring to book.)* How about physician assisted?

ROSE: Oh, I don't want to go to Switzerland, all that fresh mountain air and cuckoo clocks. I don't want to die abroad. And just think how difficult it would be, you getting the body back.

CAMILLE: Am I the only one having trouble with this conversation?

ED: It happens here anyway, unofficially. Only they call it 'making them more comfortable', with a heavy hand on the pain relief, and away they slip.

ROSE: And why not? Why drag it out when you can see the exit sign?

MAUREEN: You wouldn't leave a dog in its misery.

ROSE: Exactly. So put it through the statute books.

MAUREEN: But the trick is in knowing whether the dog's in misery or not.
As far as some are concerned, I've been in misery my entire life. It's a miracle I'm still here.

CAMILLE notices MAUREEN is trying to bring the chair to a central, dominating position. She crosses, takes the chair from MAUREEN and returns it to the far side of the room, just out of the door into the garden. MAUREEN turns around and begins to make her way back to the chairs.

ISABELLA: In Contemporary Society at school, our teacher said the first thing they've done in every state and country that's brought in physician assisted suicide is cut back on medical care and benefits for the disabled and terminally ill.

MAUREEN: Not better living, but easier dying. It's always the bruised fruit – which is often the sweetest – that gets thrown away first.

ISABELLA: It's financially beneficial.

MAUREEN: Not for the poor sods given no option but:

She mimes slitting her own throat, hanging herself, and giving herself a fatal injection.

Chuck the useless eaters overboard to better balance the economic ship of the state.

MAUREEN continues trying to reinstate her Mother's wingchairs, exiting to the garden and dragging them back in. It's a duet of sorts. Each time shere introduces a chair, CAMILLE stops decorating and efficiently removes it again.

ISABELLA: When you look at it, there's actually not much left for younger generations. We're top heavy with oldies and greedy baby boomers gobbling everything in the nest.

CAMILLE: Excuse me?

ISABELLA: If the law changed and older people thought it was their moral duty to make space for the rest of us, there'd be houses and jobs – and we'd save a fortune on geriatric care, never mind state pensions.

ED: I do hope she's not going into politics.

CAMILLE: 'Oh dear I'm in the way. I and my shrivelled ovaries are no use anymore, so I'd better get on with shuffling off this mortal coil so you can have my job along with the life insurance.'

ED: You'd be made to feel like a burden –

ROSE: I'd feel liberated, knowing I could die safely, with dignity, when I chose.

ED: – like you had to get out of the way so as not to be a drain on the family.

CAMILLE: And they always use this supposedly empowering language: *'Choice. Autonomy. Moral right to control one's body.'*

ROSE: Quite right. It's my body. I shall do what I want with it.

CAMILLE: So long as you're not manipulated, or the rights get abused.

ISABELLA: Why do we always assume that's going to happen?

MAUREEN: Give us an inch and we'll be out bumping off granny before you can say morphine overdose.

ISABELLA: Are people really so bad?

ROSE: Apparently at heart we're all scheming murderers with a liking for eugenics, or weak victims who need the law to protect us from our dark and grasping natures.

CAMILLE: *(Considering her paintwork.)* I was right the first time. I should have done Semolina, not Burnt Sienna.

ED: Or tapioca, crème brulee, spotted dick, arctic roll?

ISABELLA: 'Every man has a right to risk his own life in order to preserve it.'

CAMILLE: Dear God.

ISABELLA: That's Rousseau's Social Contract. We did him last term.

CAMILLE: What do they teach you in that school?

ISABELLA: To think.

ROSE: That's what you're paying for. If you wanted her to be a drudge you could've put her through the local school.

ED: Or kept her at home, with a whole rota of illnesses. Unusually experienced in alphabetical order according to the index of the Home Medical Encyclopaedia…

ROSE: Yes, you were a sickly child. So demanding. Always an arse or elbow wrong with you.

ED: Which never stopped me peeling the spuds. Or changing the beds. Or scrubbing the floor, down on my hands and knees.

ROSE: And such a remarkable imaginative inner life. I suppose it came from fever. Hallucinations from high temperatures.

(Beat.)

ISABELLA: In my Living Ethics After School Club we're doing Kant. He looks at the act only, not the consequences or outcomes. Basically, he argues a person can't be used merely as a means, but must in all actions be considered as an end in themselves. Therefore it would be unethical to commit suicide to satisfy oneself.

MAUREEN: So what about masturbation, then? I suppose for Kant a wank is out of the question?

ISABELLA: Hello, I'm still here!

ED: Don't you get tired of hearing all these men? Where's the women?

CAMILLE: *(Taking chair off MAUREEN.)* At home baking cookies and trying to put their heads in the oven at the same time.

ED: Why are you always quoting men?

ISABELLA: Because no one takes me seriously.

ROSE: And do you think we ever will if you're just an echo, bouncing back what someone with a penis and a beard said? Cultivate your own voice and ideas; it's the only way you'll truly grow.

(Beat.)

You know what I find fascinating? You both seem opposed to my wish, yet neither of you has asked me why I want to do it.

ED & CAMILLE: Mother: Why do you want to do it?

ROSE: Because life has lost its value and meaningfulness.

CAMILLE: Oh, Christ, she'll be scrutinising her navel next…

ROSE: I said *meaningfulness*, not meaning. I know the meaning of life.

ISABELLA: Which is –?

ROSE: Why, Death, of course, darling.
But I'm also pragmatic. I've spent fifty years clinging onto this house and I'll be damned if I have to sell it just to pay for my care. Because that's what coming, you know that, don't you? And how ironic would that be? Your inheritance squandered to pay for a nursing home I don't want to be in, patronised and dressed in communal clothing, not even my own knickers, kept in the world when I'd really rather leave it. Put like that, I rather thought you'd be supportive of my wishes.

CAMILLE: Well it's certainly very logical…

ISABELLA: Mam!

CAMILLE: Well it is!

ED: Sometimes I can't believe we're related.

ROSE: Oh, hush, all of you. I'm seventy-six and I feel a hundred years old. It's not going to improve, so let's cut to the chase and make an early night of it.

ISABELLA: Well, I'd hardly say seventy-six was *early*…

ROSE: It's like a film. You've sat through more than half of it and it's been terrible, deeply disappointing, and unlikely to get good at the end, to make the whole painful experience worthwhile. So what do you do?

ISABELLA: Walk out?

ROSE: Exactly.

ED: But what if it does?

ROSE: What?

ED: Get good right at the end? What if something spectacular happens at the closing that gives meaning to what came before?

ROSE: I had you down as a depressive and pessimist. I take it back.

ED: Like a punch line in a joke – you've no idea what's funny or significant until you see how it ends.

ROSE: But I know how it will end. With dignity, at a time of my choosing, in a manner we have yet to identify.

ISABELLA: How about Russian roulette?

ROSE: Ah, guns… It is better to shoot yourself in the back of the head rather than the temple. Easily done, an easy mistake. Van Gogh painted three canvases in the time it took him to die after shooting himself in the wrong place, poor dab. And don't for god's sake put the gun in your mouth; you'll only shoot your jaw away and that will make any surviving years miserable, as no one will know what you're talking about and you'll have to liquefy everything and be fed through a tube – a terrible affliction if one of your few remaining comforts is eating. No, through the back of the head, behind the right ear is best, and with a 38 Calibre revolver.

CAMILLE: Who do you think you are, Clint Eastwood?

CAMILLE emphatically removes the chair MAUREEN has been reintroducing. Worn out, MAUREEN gives up, heading slowly for the exit into the rest of the house.

MAUREEN: Don't forget the wadcutter target bullets, the Sheriff was very clear about that.

CAMILLE: Sheriff?

ROSE: Oh yes. They're specially designed for shooting paper targets – they have a flat front that cuts a very clean hole.

CAMILLE: Sheriff?

ROSE: Yes, dear and I don't mean of Nottingham, but the Midwest. It's amazing whom you can befriend online: sheriffs, survivalists, evangelicals, First Nation people. I've had some fascinating discussions. Apparently, the Dakota Native Americans believe that the ghost of a suicide forever drags the tree on which they swung behind them.

CAMILLE: Does it put them off?

ROSE: No. They just look for very small trees.

GLORIA enters. She watches MAUREEN closely as they pass, MAUREEN exits.

ROSE: Oh look, it's Mother Teresa of Costcutters. Is it very trying for you, slumming it down here with us heathens?

GLORIA: I didn't even say a word.

ROSE: You don't need to. Your face – so expressive – it speaks volumes.

GLORIA: Shall I go out and come in again?

ROSE: I'm sorry darling. I don't know what's got into me today. I'm like a nettle. I'd sting you.

GLORIA: I've been out, walking.

ED: Cruising the neighbourhood, checking out the old haunts?

GLORIA: A walking meditation.

CAMILLE: Can I ask your opinion? What do you think of colour?

GLORIA: We're all the same, black, pink, yellow, beige, from the same creator, the same source, the –

CAMILLE: – No, on the walls. The colour. Consider it in relationship to the housing crisis, economic downturn, and general unrest throughout the world…

GLORIA: Excuse me?

CAMILLE: I'm saying this to my clients all the time: Our homes are our havens, and personal, political and cultural events impact on how we want that haven to be. This is reflected in the colour we paint on our walls. At the moment we want the equivalent of macaroni cheese – something traditional, comforting, full of carbs – but with the occasional pop of acid yellow or crimson as accent pieces to suggest we're ultimately hopeful about the future. So what do you think? About the walls?

GLORIA: In truth?

CAMILLE: Of course.

GLORIA: I preferred how it was, before.

ROSE: Told you.

CAMILLE: So, looking at it – what are your associations?

GLORIA: Projectile vomiting. Diarrhea.

CAMILLE: Not the effect I was after.

GLORIA: In fact, if you weren't suicidal before, I think you'd want to take your life after spending time in here.

ROSE: *(Looking at walls.)* Interesting.

GLORIA: That was a joke? My way of saying despite what's going on with Mother, maybe we can still have a laugh and remind ourselves why life is so worth living.

ROSE: Pass me the tablets.

Beat. GLORIA looks at all the books lying about.

GLORIA: What's with all the books? When we were growing up, we had the Littlewoods catalogue, The Watch Tower and

GLORIA, ED & CAMILLE: 'Valley of the Dolls'

GLORIA: under the cushion

CAMILLE: of the chair in the parlour!

(They laugh, delighted.)

You remember that?

GLORIA: I thought it was my secret.

CAMILLE: Likewise. Where did it come from?

ED: Me.

GLORIA & CAMILLE: No!

CAMILLE: It was certainly well-thumbed.

GLORIA: It's where I got my sex education from.

ED: And there's me thinking you were a natural.

GLORIA: We were feral – knew nothing – we had to find out about things somehow.

CAMILLE: God you were fast –

GLORIA: I think the word is 'easy'. Sign of low self-esteem.

CAMILLE: – everyone was mad about you.

GLORIA: I'd go with anyone for a kind word.

CAMILLE: The boys at school put up with me just because I was your sister. Hoped I might recommend them, or something.

GLORIA: Well, there were enough of them over the years.

ROSE: Don't we know it.

ED: You had my portion, too.

CAMILLE: And most of the local population's.

GLORIA: Why was that allowed to happen?

ED: What, you becoming the village bike?

ROSE: Now-now.

GLORIA: Why didn't someone intervene?

CAMILLE: You were invincible!

ROSE: You knew your own mind.

GLORIA: I was little more than a child! Why didn't anyone put me in line?

CAMILLE: No one would dare. You were fearsome! Take the face off anyone soon as look at them. Even the teachers were scared of you. You'd saunter down the school corridor, hips swaying, a halo of hair around your face like a lion's mane… Glorious…

ED: Glorious Gloria.

CAMILLE: That was it, yes. Glorious Gloria.

A moment of sweetness, then sadness of time passing and the distance between them all. A change. GLORIA *drops her head. A beat.*
Her eye is caught by one of the open books littering the floor. She reads:

GLORIA: 'Mixing Clorox and ammonia produces lethal chlorine gas…'

(She takes up the book, turns some pages.)

'Senecol is considered the Rolls Royce of despatch drugs which, when combined with alcohol and sleeping pills …'
What's going on here?

ROSE: None of your business. You weren't invited. It was breaking and entering, you coming into my house.

GLORIA: The door was open.

ROSE: So is that an invitation to any stranger off the road –

GLORIA: I'm your daughter, flesh and blood.

ROSE: So act like it.

GLORIA: I've a good mind to report this.

CAMILLE: To whom, for what?

ISABELLA: We're just reading.

GLORIA: Your child is involved in this?

ISABELLA: They're just words.

CAMILLE: All we want to know when determining how to die is what's legal or not.

GLORIA: But that's not your call – determining how or when to die. It's none of your choice or power to do this.

ROSE: Isn't it? The only thing I own is myself; the only thing I can completely lay claim to is my body. I will dispose of it as I wish.

GLORIA: But it's not yours. It's in keeping, that's all; it's been loaned to you and you should treat it respectfully, as you would any possession that's been left in your care. Only the creator knows or decides when to call you home.

ED: 'Come in, number 33, your time's up.'

ROSE: So what happens when there's no creator but myself? You know I don't believe in a higher power, and I certainly don't believe that my flesh has been loaned to me. I am the author of my own story

GLORIA: – so continue being that by listening to what life is trying to tell you, directing your own treatment, taking charge.

ROSE: That's what I'm doing.

GLORIA: No you're not. You're caving in. You're giving up.

ROSE: Dying is not giving up. It's dying.

GLORIA: You can't give up just because you're tired or unhappy or –

ROSE: What about being in pain? Or grief? In terror? The fear of losing control? How about for that future little plastic tube protruding from my back to drain the poison from my kidneys? How about to avoid watching you watch me fade away? Or avoiding the incontinence and the hallucinations, where I could be screaming COCKROACHES! COCKROACHES! convinced they're crawling all over me and there's nothing you or anyone else can do?
How about to avoid a living death?
Don't you understand? I don't want to give up my life in order to live.

GLORIA: But it's an opportunity for growth, for understanding, for –

ROSE: You know I don't believe there's value in suffering. It doesn't bring spirituality, or depth to character, or nobility. I'm not buying into those bonuses for the hereafter, for there isn't one. It's only a hole in the ground and compost. That's it.

(She begins to leave.)

GLORIA: I'm dying.

(ROSE continues walking away.)

Mother, I'm dying.

(ROSE stops.)

And I think it wrong – I think it is so wrong to be indulging your talk of ending it all when you're competent and relatively healthy. I want to live but I don't have that CHOICE. So don't tell me it's fine and dandy to CHOOSE how to die, because I want to live, only I don't have the luxury of CHOICE.

(Several beats.)

ROSE: It's daddy's illness, isn't it? The same as what your father had. From him, through me.

GLORIA: You can't even say its name.

CAMILLE: Really?

GLORIA: As if I'd lie about this…

(Beat.)

CAMILLE: How long have you known?

GLORIA: A while.

(Beat.)

ROSE: I'm sorry.

GLORIA: What use is your sorrow to me?

ROSE: No use.
No use at all.

ROSE continues to exit.

End of scene.

FIVE

Late. A sleeping house. Quietly and in low light, CAMILLE is speed walking around the room. She finishes a circuit, touches her hipbone, then checks the app on her phone. Clearly not yet the 10,000 daily steps, she sets off again. Bored, she starts playing with her phone. She tries and fails to play a app game whilst walking, attempts to check email but there's no signal. Bored, she speed walks, looking about the room, then starts recording her voice.

CAMILLE: Highly desirable, generous family accommodation. An exciting opportunity for this superbly presented, charming and unique villa in an excellent little sought-after position, far away from any school, amenity or place where anyone in their right mind would want to live… A stunning example of urban decay...echoing the elegance of neoclassical design, without delivering clean lines or indeed anything even remotely hygienic, this bewildering melange of styles, incompetence, and residual family trauma will have any prospective buyer running for the hills or doubting their good sense for coming here in the first place…

She notices several of the wingchairs have made it back into the room and goes over to remove one – then sees a pair of legs sticking out. Someone sleeping, covered by a blanket. Quietly she exits.

Several beats. Two figures enter, ROSE and MAUREEN. ROSE holds a pamphlet and large plastic bag with ice wrapped in a teacloth inside it – she checks the prone figure is asleep – then gently places the bag loosely over prone figure's head. She gingerly tries to make the bag less loose at the neck, folding it over, pleating it, but air is still going in. She wavers, summons courage, then steps back, letting MAUREEN do it. MAUREEN begins to tighten the bag, twisting the end at the prone figure's neck. ROSE begins:

ROSE: Go into the light. The light. Move towards the light. It's dark, you're in a tunnel, but move into the light, move into the light…

Suddenly the figure jerks, arms flailing, making muffled cries, fighting to tear MAUREEN's hands and the bag away. MAUREEN cocks a leg and puts her full weight onto the struggling figure as ROSE intones:

ROSE: It's beautiful. All your pain and suffering, gone. You're almost there, crossing over. Your Buddha, your Jesus, your Everything is there – in the light – there – this dazzling, warming, welcoming light.

The figure is really struggling now. MAUREEN and ROSE hold them down.

You can let go. Just surrender, merge with the universe, you're particles of stars – just –

Prone figure manages to tear the bag off, gasps with breath. It is ED.

ED: Jesus! Jesus!

The light switches on. CAMILLE stands in her dressing gown, a raised walking stick in her hand. She takes in the scene. All are frozen, silent, stunned.

A beat.

ROSE: So that's *not* how we're going to do it.

ED: Fucking hell. You nearly killed me.

MAUREEN: That's the general idea, but no – I made holes in the bag, you weren't ever really at risk.

ED: You try telling my lungs, my heart that! And what's with the ice? It was freezing!

ROSE: That's to keep the temperature inside the bag from becoming too uncomfortable.

ED: You're bloody dying! Surely there's going to be some discomfort?

ROSE: Not if you do it right and that's why we're practising. That is how not to do it. That is how it will not happen. No intoning. No 'moving into the light', no calls for god or Buddha or the fairies at the bottom of the garden, no waiting until the moment of loss of consciousness before slipping the hood of deliverance over the head.

ED: The hood – ?!

ROSE: *(Referring to 'Do Yourself In' pamphlet.)* 'It should be in place after the lethal dose of drugs but before loss of consciousness and preferably done by the escapee themselves whilst still alert and aware and owning the situation.' People panic if they start falling asleep and someone puts a bag over their head –

ED: I noticed.

ROSE: – so if it's done when conscious, right at the start, it's usually fine. *(Looking at diagram in pamphlet.)* And it's placed over the head with these rubber bands at the neck, held with the fingers, so as unconsciousness comes, the fingers slacken, the elastic tightens, the bag seals and eventually you just drift away, gone from oxygen deprivation, not suffocation or choking. So there should be no struggle, no unpleasant surprises, no loss of dignity…

ED: How can dying with a fucking Tesco Bag for Life over your head be dignified?

ROSE: That's true.

MAUREEN: It's removed, afterwards.

ROSE: But it's during, during the actual moment… It's not how I expected. I imagined it differently… Arvo Part in the background

CAMILLE: Christ.

ROSE: and the smell of freesias –

ED: – which you wouldn't smell or hear anyway, because of the freezing bag of ice over your bloody head!

GLORIA arrives in a state of hurried dress…

GLORIA: I heard shouting. What on earth is going on here?

ROSE: Nothing. Nothing that concerns you, darling. It's fine.

ED: She almost killed me with a plastic bag.

GLORIA: What?!

ED: You say that's nothing? It's fine?

MAUREEN: It was just a dry run. Rehearsing.

ED: You might have warned me. Asked my permission?

ROSE: Don't be silly, darling, that would ruin the element of surprise and we needed an authentic reaction, to see if we can handle it, or need more help.

ED: The way I feel at the moment, Mother, I could quite happily help kill you – in fact, I'd do it all by myself, with the greatest of pleasure.

ROSE: That's the spirit.

ED leaves with a parting furious glance at MAUREEN, who starts heading, as usual, towards the garden, pulling her catheter behind her. As they exit, both slam the doors behind them.

GLORIA: I can't believe you did that.

ROSE: Well how I am supposed to know what it's like unless I try a dry run?

CAMILLE: It's all about you, isn't it?

ROSE: In the hierarchy of family issues, I imagine an exit plan is pretty high – even higher than bankruptcy and unemployment, wouldn't you say? All you need to do is bide your time, and you'll get what you want.

GLORIA: What you just did to Ed –

ROSE: – She's fine, you molly-coddle her too much. You forget, we've been living together all her life. After so many decades of co-dependent loathing, you reach an understanding.

CAMILLE: Well if you hate life and your children so much, perhaps you should go on ahead and end it.

ROSE: Darling, I don't hate you or life. I want you to remember me in my prime, not be traumatised seeing me with an indignity I can't cover up. Can't you see this as a tragic affirmation? Life means so much to me, I will not settle for anything else and I will not accept a living death as substitute.

CAMILLE: What 'living death'?

GLORIA: You're in such conflict with your body, and what may happen.
Be here now.

ROSE: But you don't know…(what it's like.)

GLORIA: I do know what it's like. And if the disease is the enemy we're either its victim or attacker. Where's the peace in that?

ROSE: I don't want it – that line in the sand –

CAMILLE: What line?

ROSE: The one that keeps moving. The 'I'd rather die than lose my looks' – and it starts happening and suddenly beauty is more than skin deep. Or 'the day I can't feed or wash myself is the day I check out' – and I see them nappied-up and spoon fed, thinking this isn't perhaps so bad after all. Then the 'I'll kill myself before I lose all control and can't do it for myself' – and suddenly they're trapped in a useless body that can't even count out the pills or open the packet of Gillette – and that's that – the moving line which keeps moving. Not for me. It stops here and now. I've my will and casket all ready. All I need to do is set a date.

CAMILLE: Make it sound like you're planning a wedding or car boot sale, why don't you?

GLORIA: You're ending your life prematurely because you're governed by fear.

ROSE: And you think believing in Mr Blobby, or Buddha, or Jesus, or whoever is going to help?

GLORIA: What?

ROSE: With your dying. You think this higher power is going to make it easier?

GLORIA: Yes. I know it.

ROSE: And you're sure it's not just the illness?

CAMILLE: Stop.

ROSE: This 'blinding insight'…

CAMILLE: Mother…

ROSE: Sounds like a symptom to me, or side effects from drugs.

GLORIA: I can't control the events that happen in my life. I can't control what happens to me at a genetic level, but I can have a say in how I perceive it, how I respond.
Life is short and precious.

GLORIA leaves. CAMILLE follows her.
ROSE sits in the quiet.
Several beats.
MAUREEN enters from the garden, without her catheter.

MAUREEN: It's stopped. The passing blood, it seems to have stopped.

(Beat.)

I don't know if it's a good or a bad thing.

ROSE: Could be either. Could be both.

MAUREEN: Because if it's good – I mean – if it's stopped, they can maybe…? Who knows – but it might suggest…
I'm sorry.
I need to find out. Because if there's a chance –

ROSE: Yes.

MAUREEN: – I have to…

ROSE: Of course.

MAUREEN: I love being alive.

ROSE: I'm happy for you.

MAUREEN: No, you're not.
But I'm in it for the long haul; the adventure of seeing what part of me fails next.

She passes through towards the front door.

The main thing is never to lose heart. Other things – teeth, virtue, handbags, memories – they can be lost. But not the heart. To lose heart is… to invite despair. And we all know what that means, don't we?

She continues out, the front door closing behind her.
ROSE is left alone. She sits, listening to the silence, not sure what to do.
Time passes.
She picks up one of the books and reads:

ROSE: 'They tell us that suicide is the greatest act of cowardice…that suicide is wrong, when it is quite obvious that there is nothing in the world to which every man has a more unassailable title than to his own life and person.' Schopenhauer.

ISABELLA's voice emerges, but she is unseen.

ISABELLA: 'If freedom is self-ownership, the right to end that life is the most basic of all. If others force you to live, you belong to them and don't own yourself.' Thomas Szazz.

ROSE: 'The thought of suicide is a great consolation. By means of it

ISABELLA & ROSE: one gets successfully through many a bad night.'

ISABELLA: Nietzsche.

ISABELLA pops her head up from one of the wing chairs reinstated at the back of the room.

Do you intend on being alive at Christmas?

ROSE: I don't know.

ISABELLA: Well – if you're here at Christmas, I suppose I'll see you then.

ROSE: What a strange fish you are.

ISABELLA: Yes. But my mother says I have caviar inside me.

ROSE: She would.

ISABELLA: Yes. Because she loves me.

ROSE: Darling, this has all been about love.

ISABELLA leaves.
ROSE sits. It is very quiet.
Time passes.

ROSE: What does it amount to – a life? The number of cards you get at Christmas? The number of funerals you go to? Another in the earth. Yet another up in flames. You can stand outside crematoriums and watch the smoke, rising. Is that all we are? Stuff for the bonfire? And will someone turn off that sentimental music? Or put a gun to my head when I go off on this drivel? Somebody?

ED enters from the shadows.

ED: I dream sometimes a giant sinkhole has opened up right across the front path, and the whole house is tipping forward into it. And I'm there at the door, my toes curled under me, gripping, trying to keep my balance and not go head-first –and there's nothing, nothing beneath me –
And sometimes at night when I'm walking the corridors, just wandering around in the small hours, the house is a burnt out planet, a dark star, and I'm alone. I'm always alone.

ROSE: Oh, goose…

ED: I'm just saying, I'm just –

ROSE: I'm sorry darling. I think it's time you left home.

ED: I don't think I can.

ROSE: You put one foot in front of the other and slam the door behind you.

ED: I don't want to leave you.

ROSE: You're not, darling.
Perhaps I'm leaving you.
And besides, your sisters need you.

ED takes her time, but eventually leaves.
The door closes behind her.
ROSE is alone.

To despair is to be buried alive, embalmed, but the heart's still ticking. Those quiet hours of the night when you're there, waiting for dawn. Waiting for the first trace of light, scanning the sky, praying, holding your breath almost, willing the light oh do not let me fall into darkness, do not let me

You try walking across a room when it feels like scaling a vertical wall, clinging by fingernails in cracks. At times I wanted to go on all fours – Inching my way along the wall, from bedroom to bathroom, hugging the ground, slithering along the face of the earth like a parasite. That's all. A worm. Less. Darkness comes, sweeping up like an incoming tide. And at times I thought I was buried in the water, its waves over my head – that muffled silence at 3 A.M. – feeling the pump pump pump of your heart, the fear, and the jaw going, any nonsense, any rubbish, anything just not to let the silence in, not let the pause fill, to keep jawing and mouthing

You think it's an easy thing. You only see the service, the funeral, the washed body in the chapel of rest, the candles. You haven't seen the terror, the clawing at life, as though slipping into a hole, quicksand, fingers clawing in the loose earth at the edge of the pit, the desperation, the –

You think it's fine and a fearless thing, a natural progression, life to death, cradle to grave. You think it's natural and easy.

There is nothing gentle about death. There is nowhere to take your ease, just the scrabbling, the terrible scrabbling of fingers in the earth, the clawing, the fear and all the time thinking: who'll be there to hold my hand when my turn comes?

Hold my hand.

Someone?

A line of the chairs become visible at the back, with ISABELLA, CAMILLE, ED, GLORIA and MAUREEN sitting in them. They watch ROSE.

Let me not fall into darkness
Ssssh…
No no no no not into the dark, not into the dark, please –
Ssssh
Cosy, cosy. It comes, it comes
Not into the dark!
Stars. Stars.

Blackout.

End of play.

www.ingramcontent.com/pod-product-compliance
Ingram Content Group UK Ltd.
Pitfield, Milton Keynes, MK11 3LW, UK
UKHW031249020325
455689UK00008B/146

9 781783 193172